Niles Public Library District
6960 Oakton Street • Niles, Illinois 60714
Phone 847-663-1234

VIETNAM

MODERN
NATIONS
—OF THE—
WORLD

VIETNAM

BY KAREN WILLS

LUCENT BOOKS
P.O. BOX 289011
SAN DIEGO, CA 92198-9011

JUL 2000

Library of Congress Cataloging-in-Publication Data

Wills, Karen.
   Vietnam / by Karen Wills.
      p.   cm. — (Modern nations of the world)
Includes bibliographical references and index.
Summary: Examines the land, people, and history of Vietnam and discusses
its current state of affairs and place in the world today.
   ISBN 1-56006-635-0 (lib. : alk. paper)
   1. Vietnam—Juvenile literature.   [1. Vietnam.]   I. Title.   II. Series.
   DS556.3 .W55   2000
   959.704'4—dc21

                                                                99-050957

CONTENTS

INTRODUCTION
A LAND OF TRADITION AND TRANSITION

In Vietnam's capital city, Hanoi, rushing vehicles—motorcycles, cars, and buses—stream past streetside vendors selling everything from pho, the noodle soup popular for breakfast, to fresh bouquets of colorful flowers. Jewelry, ceramic elephants, postcards, T-shirts, and even live birds and animals are all for sale on the streets of Vietnam's urban centers. There, the din of horns penetrates family-owned specialty shops, the offices of international businesses, and apartments, some large, but many tiny and crowded. Like Ho Chi Minh City in the southern region, Hanoi has undergone massive physical growth and economic change in the last century.

In the quiet, green countryside, however, peasant life continues to follow the ancient cycles of planting and harvesting

Peasants tend rice paddies near Nha Trang, Vietnam.

rice. Even with the installation of electricity in village homes, which has brought outside influences such as television, rural life in Vietnam has changed less in recent years than urban life. Traditional activities, such as celebrating festivals, tending ancestral burial plots, or worshiping at the ancestral altar in the center of the home, mark peasant life today as they have for centuries.

In the city, traditional rituals such as burning incense at the ancestral altar of the home are still observed, but lifestyles are more varied and more flexible now than in the past. In the city, women still wear the traditional *ao dai*, a high-necked, fitted tunic with panels that flow to the knees over loose-fitting trousers. Often, though, young Vietnamese women exchange the ao dai for Western dress. Today a young woman might casually ride on the back of a boyfriend's motorcycle and spend an evening in a disco, dancing. A generation earlier, such freedoms would not have been permitted, as women were strictly chaperoned during courtship.

Historically, the Vietnamese have resisted foreign influences in order to preserve their identity as a people and an

Vietnam's cities are urban centers where visitors can find everything from jewelry to live birds.

independent nation. Even when world powers intervened in Vietnam, these giants were driven out by the sheer cunning and determination of the Vietnamese. However, foreign influence, once introduced, has inevitably become entangled with Vietnamese history and culture.

This intermingling of many cultures, added to Vietnam's own rich heritage, defines Vietnam today. Vietnamese who cherish traditional features of their culture such as a strong sense of community and cooperation, respect for elders, and close family ties, seek harmony between traditional values and the pursuit of commercial/technological advancement. Vietnam is a country of traditions in an exciting time of transition. In this era of peace and freedom from foreign domination, there is room for hope that a balance of old and new cultural ways can be found.

THE GEOGRAPHY AND CLIMATE OF VIETNAM

The Socialist Republic of Vietnam, shaped like a graceful S, forms the eastern edge of the Indochinese peninsula in Southeast Asia. Bordering the S, pressed against its back, are the nations of Laos and Cambodia. Vietnam shares its northern border with China. Vietnam's eastern coastline faces the Gulf of Tonkin in the North, the South China Sea in the center, and the Gulf of Thailand in the South, three seas that together form the western edge of the Pacific Ocean.

The ends of the S fan out and flatten. At the north and south ends of the country are two fertile deltas, or alluvial plains, the ideal environment for the green paddies of Vietnam that produce one-third of the world's rice. Plenty of water and a large labor force make it possible for farmers to harvest three rice crops a year.

The Vietnamese mainland is 127,242 miles in area, about the size of the state of Washington. At its narrowest point, in the thin center, Vietnam is only about 31 miles wide. Its greatest width is 372 miles.

Historically and geographically, Vietnam is often viewed as three regions: North (BacBo), Central (Trung Bo), and South (Nam Bo). Each region has distinctive features, but all three have been influenced by water—water in the form of rain, rivers, and sea.

Vietnam claims as its territory a sea area three times as large as its landmass. This area includes the Gulf of Tonkin, the South China Sea, and the Gulf of Thailand, overlooked by the northern, central, and southern coastlines, respectively.

These three small seas are dotted with more than a thousand islands. Vietnam's possession of some of these islands is in dispute, however, as China too claims the Paracel Islands and the Sprately Islands, both in the South China Sea. Neither group of islands has great value in itself, but the country that has sovereignty over them can also lay claim to a large section of the South China Sea, said to be rich in oil reserves. Potential profits from commercial exploitation make the islands and the waters around them a prize worth pursuing.

In the past, Vietnam's coastline attracted profit-hungry traders, who saw Vietnam as rich in resources and, with its long coastline, vulnerable to conquest. Today, with Vietnam at peace, its coastline can be appreciated for its beauty and biological diversity and abundance.

Equally beautiful are Vietnam's mountains. As geographic features, they have defined Vietnam and influenced its people's

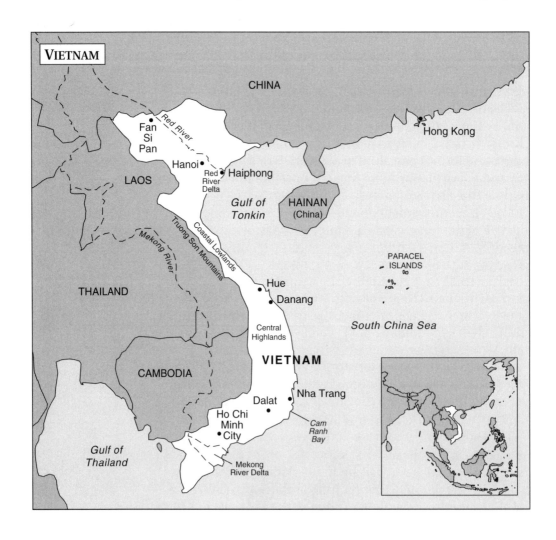

lives and history nearly as much as the rivers and sea. Three-quarters of the country is mountainous, but because this wild terrain is much less hospitable to human habitation than the coastal regions, less than one-third of the total population, mostly ethnic minority tribes, live there.

The Red River (shown here) is one of Vietnam's most important waterways.

FEATURES OF THE NORTH

As do mountains, rivers define the scenery and lifestyles of the Vietnamese. The Red River in the North and the Mekong in the South are both vital waterways.

Flowing into Vietnam from China, the Red River is named for the red silt it gathers on its journey. From the limestone cliffs of the Hoang Lien Son mountain range, the river runs through Hanoi, the country's capital city, to the lively trading port of Haiphong, where it flows into the Gulf of Tonkin.

As the Red River reaches the lower country near the sea, it spreads out to form a fertile delta. The soil-enriching silt deposits of the delta enable its largely farming population to produce more than ample rice crops for both domestic consumption and export.

Unfortunately, the people of these watery lowlands must also cope with regular flooding during the wet season, which often brings destructive storms known as monsoons. To prevent devastation from floods, a series of dikes is maintained along the rivers. Dikes have also been constructed to prevent soil and crop damage caused by inundation of salty seawater during high tides. American journalist and student of Asian culture Susan Brownmiller writes:

> There are those who say that of all the factors that conspired to make the Vietnamese so enduring, the most important was the continual struggle against the floodwaters

★ YEAR-ROUND MONSOONS

Vietnam lies in the monsoon zone of Southeast Asia. Monsoons, great seasonal winds, determine the country's weather in rhythmic cycles, bringing moisture to nourish junglelike vegetation even where the soil is poor. The winter monsoon arrives from the northeast between October and March, bringing wet, chilly weather to the northern two-thirds of the country and making the southern third warm and dry.

During the other half of the year, from April or May until October, the southwestern winds arrive, bringing moisture gathered during the crossing of the Indian Ocean and Gulf of Thailand. The summer monsoon brings warmth and humidity to the entire country with the exceptions of the central coast lowlands, which are blocked from the wind by mountains, and the Red River Delta far to the north.

Monsoon clouds form over the Mekong Delta.

to provide a sufficiency of grain, because it instructed a hardy, determined people in the sensitive art of working together.[1]

A boat travels Halong Bay, one of the most scenic areas in Vietnam.

While the waters of the Red River are vital to agriculture, the coastal waters of the northern region form a unique junction of sea and shore that draws trade and tourism. Above the port city of Haiphong, the spectacular northern coastline is marked by limestone walls that seem to rise straight up from the Gulf of Tonkin. Halong Bay, one of the most scenic areas of the gulf, is dotted with limestone islands—some in the form of peaks, some as rounded hills—that feature misty coves and caverns housing fantastic mineral formations. A former hideout for pirates, Halong Bay is now a favorite boating trip for tourists.

South of Haiphong are the flat plains of the Red River Delta region. This lowland area is the most heavily populated in Vietnam, with an average density of one thousand people per square mile. With so many people packed together, it is not surprising that the region's narrow beaches are neither clean nor considered attractive to tourists.

THE MOUNTAINS OF THE NORTH

But the North is far from being uniformly flat. The highest peaks in all of Indochina are in the Hoang Lien Son range in northern Vietnam; some exceed 9,800 feet, including Fansipan, the highest at 10,312 feet. Almost vertical slopes, peaks even the best mountain climbers cannot scale, and plunging ravines have made this range a natural barrier to attack from the north. The last attempted Chinese invasion took place in 1979, but Vietnamese troops forced the Chinese back across the border by meeting them in battle in the harsh terrain of the northern mountains.

MINERAL RESOURCES

The harsh northern terrain is balanced by a wealth of minerals such as anthracite coal, iron ore, copper, lead, zinc, bauxite, chrome, titanium, gold, tungsten and tin, gemstones, and quartz. Phosphate, a key ingredient in much of the world's processed fertilizer, is abundant. The country also produces fine clay for porcelain.

Since the late 1980's, when Vietnam's communist government opened the country to private investment, more money to develop this wealth of resources has become available. Royal Dutch Shell, British Petroleum, and Australia's Broken Hill Proprietary, for example, along with American companies, are all studying or negotiating the rights to offshore exploratory drilling for oil and natural gas.

THE CLIMATE OF THE NORTH

Just as Vietnam's natural resources vary from region to region, so does its climate. All of Vietnam is in the tropical zone, but weather patterns are not uniform. In the North, there are four distinct seasons. Northern winters last from November to April, during which time temperatures in the mountains can drop below freezing. January is the coldest month, when Hanoi's average temperature is 61.7 degrees Fahrenheit. Especially in February and March, people in the northern region live with drizzling rain, which they call "rain dust." Humid year round, Hanoi is hottest in the summer months. The average June temperature in Hanoi is 83.8 degrees Fahrenheit.

THE CITADEL

Hue is the site of the famous fortlike ruins known as the Citadel on the east bank of the Perfume River. Emperor Gia Long began its construction in 1802. A formidable combination of French- and Chinese-inspired design, the Citadel served as the administrative center for the nation until 1945.

The Citadel's design is a nest of three boxes surrounded by a moat. Workers and shopkeepers lived in the outer "box," mandarin scholars and bureaucrats in the palaces and gardens of the middle "box," called the Imperial City, and the royals and their servants resided in the most-protected "inside box," the Forbidden Purple City. The walls of the Citadel, designed for maximum protection range from six to thirty feet thick.

The word "Forbidden" was intended to be taken seriously. Anyone who entered the Forbidden Purple City without permission was executed. Mandarins, highly educated administrators and civil servants, paused outside the Forbidden Purple City in the Hall of Mandarins to don special clothes before entering the presence of royalty. Royal trappings were luxurious: Every meal for the emperor had to consist of fifty dishes.

During the 1968 Tet Offensive of the Vietnam War, Hue was the scene of terrible fighting as U.S. Marines fought the North Vietnamese in house-to-house combat. Much of the Citadel sustained heavy damage from ground artillery. Some military analysts believe that the fighting for Hue could have

ended sooner if the Americans had bombed the area of the Citadel. However, U.S. military planners chose not to destroy it from the air because of its historical significance to the Vietnamese.

Since the war's end, international efforts have been made, particularly through the United Nations, to restore parts of the Citadel. Until such projects are complete, the Citadel's ruins can only hint at the past glory of its palaces, theaters, libraries, pavilions, and gardens.

Once the government's administrative center, the Citadel now sits in ruins, waiting to be restored.

Clouds cover the peaks of the Troung Son Mountains, a north-to-south range that spans most of the country.

FEATURES OF THE CENTRAL REGION

As in the northern reaches of Vietnam, rivers are also vital to central Vietnam, which may be thought of as two areas—the coastal region and the Central Highlands. The mountainous Central Highlands are soaked by as much as one hundred inches of rainfall a year; such heavy precipitation contributes to flooding of the two hundred or more rivers that cut through the Central Highlands. These rivers, marked by stunning waterfalls that enhance the spectacular mountain scenery, form the waterways that serve as common transportation for the people of the region.

The central coastline of Vietnam, with its seascapes of serene blue bays and white sandy beaches, overlooks the South China Sea. In the peaceful present day, the port of Cam Ranh Bay and the town of Nha Trang attract tourism and host surfing competitions; in the past, these and other central coast locales served as recreation centers for foreign armies.

The central coast region is sprinkled with small fishing villages and a few larger towns. The old city of Hue, which rests within sight of both mountains and sea, was once a residence for Vietnamese royalty. It was also a center for Buddhist resistance activities as well as the site of terrible battles during the Vietnam War. A few miles inland from Hue is a geographic landmark of five hills known as the Marble Mountains.

A NETWORK OF MOUNTAINS

Vietnam's scenic beauty is more than the result of its coastline, or one certain mountain range. While the Hoang Lien Son range of the northern region may be the most impressive in height, it is the jungle covered Truong Son range, formerly known as the Annamite Cordilleras, that impresses with length. This range is a system of parallel mountain chains extending from north to south through nearly the entire country. Some of these chains branch off to run east to the sea, creating scenic mountain passes with romantic names such as Pass of the Clouds.

The Central Highlands comprise the southern slopes of the Truong Son mountains, falling steeply to the east, toward the sea. Between July and January much rain falls here, but during the rest of the year a southwest wind makes these uplands dry and hot. Annual rainfall is much heavier, however, on the rain forest-covered western side of the Central Highlands. These slopes extend gently into neighboring Cambodia and the Mekong River basin.

The Central Highlands are home to many seminomadic ethnic minority tribes who have traditionally lived by hunting, trapping, fishing, and slash-and-burn farming. This farming technique involves making deep cuts into the trees of a designated jungle area, thus causing the sap to dry and trees to die. Tribespeople then clear the land by setting the dead trees on fire; the resulting ash enriches the poor upland soil enough so that, for a short time, certain root crops and sticky rice will grow.

The Vietnamese government has made efforts to discourage slash-and-burn agriculture because it denudes the forests. The government has also tried to assimilate the mountain dwellers into mainstream culture, with limited success. Wary of encroachment from the lowlands, the varied tribes of the Central Highlands tend to cling to their traditional colorful costumes, languages, and lifestyles.

BOTANICAL RICHES

Besides its varied climate and diverse natural resources, Vietnam is lush in plant life, with twelve thousand species identified in its forests alone. Much flora remains unidentified, but much is known to be beneficial as medicine, food, and for commercial uses. The Central Highlands region is home

THE MARBLE MOUNTAINS

The Marble Mountains, near Danang, a coastal city south of Hue, are really limestone hills. The five hills are named after the five elements of the universe according to Chinese philosophy: water, wood, fire, metal or gold, and earth. Water, or Thuy Son, is the largest, made famous by its natural caves, which have long been used by Buddhists and Hindus for temples and shrines. Sacred shrines and statues are still part of the Marble Mountains, making them a well-known place of pilgrimage, a home to Buddhist monks, and a tourist destination.

to much of this rich plant life. Its fertile tropical rain forests are all that remain of ancient woodlands that once covered nearly all of Vietnam. The dense tropical rain forests of the Central Highlands are often referred to as the triple canopy jungle because tree growth reaches three different levels, or stories.

A government-sponsored reforestation program is in progress. Additionally, the government has prohibited the exportation of certain rare hardwoods, and has plans to set aside thousands of square kilometers as forest reserves. There is, however, some resistance to this plan from business interests, so the future preservation of forestlands in Vietnam remains uncertain.

FEATURES OF THE SOUTHERN REGION

The nation's southern region is home to the Mekong Delta. The Vietnamese name for the Mekong River, which divides into nine branches as it flows to the sea, is Cuu Long, which means River of the Nine Dragons. Vietnam historian Stanley Karnow writes of the Mekong:

Nourished by the eternal snows of Tibet, the roof of the earth, it twists and turns for nearly three thousand

Rainforests, like this one near Buon Me Thuot, once covered most of the country but now are found primarily in the Central Highlands.

Vietnam's Mekong Delta is the country's most populated area.

miles—tumbling down the rugged mountains of south-western China, cutting through the jungles of Laos . . . bending to delineate the boundary with Thailand, traversing Cambodia and finally fanning out across the delta in Vietnam before splaying into the South China Sea.[2]

The waters of the Mekong River, and the silt it carries and deposits, along with the warm, even temperatures of the South, make the Mekong Delta the richest agricultural area of Vietnam.

It is also the most densely populated area. Located just south of Ho Chi Minh City, Vietnam's largest metropolis with a population of 4 million and growing, the Mekong Delta is home to more than one-quarter of the population of Vietnam. Author and photojournalist Michael S. Yamashita, who traveled the river from its source in Tibet to its mouth in Vietnam, describes the teeming delta as "one huge green swamp crisscrossed by an intricate maze of rivers, canals, and irrigation ditches."[3] The delta produces half of all Vietnamese rice and fruit such as bananas, mangos, coconuts, and pineapples. It also provides more seafood for export than any

A cormorant perches in a restored mangrove forest in Vietnam. Since the end of the Vietnam War, the mangrove swamps have been 80 percent restored.

other area of the country. According to agronomist Va Tung Xuon, "The Mekong is the elixir of life here. They do everything in it. Drinking, working, washing and farming in it. It's our most important resource."[4]

South of the Mekong Delta, the coastal area known as the Plain of Reeds is a swamp and marshland. Its value lies in the mangroves that are native to this region. The short, knotty mangrove tree is used for medicinal oils, charcoal, building materials, and firewood.

The use of chemical agents by the U.S. military during the Vietnam War rendered this area a wasteland, but replanting since then has brought back 80 percent of the mangrove swamp. Today the swamp in the Plain of Reeds is second in size only to the world's largest mangrove swamp in the Amazon basin. But the health of the mangroves is not yet secure. Intense consumer demand for fuel and food poses a continuing threat to these wetlands as mangroves are cleared to provide the firewood that is needed for fuel and the land to build shrimp farms.

THE SOUTHERN HIGHLANDS

The South is not all delta and swamp. In the southern region, the land rises one last time to about forty-five hundred feet before giving way to lowlands. In the pine forests of these southernmost highlands, the resort town of Dalat offers a cool, scenic escape from the hot, humid summers endured by the millions who live in the Mekong Delta.

The highlands provide the only relief from southern heat. With the exception of its highest elevations, South Vietnam is sometimes wet and sometimes dry, but always hot. Ho Chi Minh City receives an annual rainfall of 80 inches, mostly between May and October. The dry season, which runs from November to April, is the city's hottest period with average temperatures exceeding 80 degrees Fahrenheit. The city's coldest temperatures come in January, when the average temperature is nevertheless a warm 78.4 degrees Fahrenheit.

REMARKABLE WILDLIFE OF VIETNAM

Vietnam's diversity is not limited to water, earth, and climate. With its profusion of rivers and varied terrain and temperatures, Vietnam is home to a remarkable variety of wildlife. The nation boasts 273 species of mammals alone, including large mammals such as the elephant, rhinoceros, and wild pig. In fact, Vietnam is one of the last places in the world where large mammals have been recently discovered. In 1993, for example, a previously unknown species, a sort of combination of cow and goat, was discovered here. Called the forest goat by peasants, it has been designated the *Pseudorix* by zoologists. Tigers, leopards and other wild cats, barking deer, black and honey bears, the piglike tapir, mountain goats, skunks, squirrels, otters, mongooses, mice, and rats live in the wild. They are joined by Vietnam's varied primate family, including baboons, rock apes, rhesus monkeys, langurs, macaques, and gibbons.

At least 180 species of reptiles are found in Vietnam, including deadly snakes. One of the most poisonous is the two-steps snake, so named because, it is said, the victim of its bite will walk only two more steps before dying. Much larger, but equally deadly, is the horse snake. Like the python, also native to Vietnam, it may grow to thirty feet.

The abundance of water in Vietnam leads to a corresponding abundance of water-dwelling wildlife. Crocodiles live in rivers, along with blood-sucking leeches. More significantly, the rivers and coastal seas of Vietnam serve as a primary food source by providing five hundred varieties of both freshwater and saltwater crab and hundreds of species of fish, as well as lobster, squid, octopus, and shrimp.

Insects breed in vast numbers in the humid tropical areas of Vietnam, including thick clouds of mosquitoes, bees, and wasps. Beetles ranging in size from nearly microscopic to several inches long turn up in stored flour and rice, and scorpions scuttle across surfaces.

The large insect population provides an ample food source for some 773 species of birds native to Vietnam. Small, brightly colored tropical birds flash through the jungles, while larger species such as black drangos, purple herons, great egrets, and sarus cranes are found in the coastal wetlands of the South.

Recognizing the value of preserving its wealth of rare wildlife such as the eastern sarus crane, Vietnam, with the help of various international organizations, established the bird sanctuary of Tram Chin, which occupies some 45,000 acres of a section of the Plain of Reeds in the South. The collective efforts at Tram Chin have brought back not only the

THE EASTERN SARUS CRANE

The crane symbolizes long life, wealth, and happiness in Asian cultures, including Vietnam's. Ironically during the Vietnam War the five-foot-tall, red-headed eastern sarus crane was nearly driven to extinction. The U.S. military, in an effort to deprive Viet Cong guerrillas of hiding places, cut drainage ditches and used napalm and other incendiary defoliants to burn away forest cover that harbored wildlife. Further imperiling the crane during that era, Vietnamese killed the bird for food and American GIs shot it for sport.

After the war, North Vietnamese and Cambodians streamed into South Vietnam. The press of human population, as well as a government reforestation program in what had been the crane's natural habitat of treeless marshlands, threatened the sarus crane's survival even more.

Now, through the existence of the bird sanctuary of Tram Chim, the eastern sarus crane has returned to its old feeding area. Each year in late December cranes arrive to stay through April, the dry season when water is shallow and the birds can walk about feeding on plants that they scratch up from the mud.

During their breeding season, the birds move across the nearby border into Cambodia. Continuing efforts to protect the eastern sarus crane may involve that country as well.

Vietnam is a virtual sanctuary for wildlife. Mammals, insects, and birds (like this egret) flourish in the open terrain.

crane but also the painted stork, black-faced spoonbill, and Bengal florican.

Vietnam, increasingly aware of the need to preserve its environment, has also established two national parks: Cuc Phuong National Park, located 87 miles southwest of Hanoi, and Nam Cat Tien National Park, 155 miles northwest of Ho Chi Minh City. Planning for more is underway.

Vietnam is trying to make the best use of its geographical features and richness of natural resources. Despite the damage caused by overuse and war, the country retains much of its natural beauty and abundant wildlife and resources. The Vietnamese people are mindful of this as they look toward the future.

2

A LAND OF
MANY INFLUENCES

The Vietnamese might be compared to a salad containing a variety of native and imported ingredients. Ethnic Vietnamese constitute about 84 percent of the population, but about 60 minority groups also call Vietnam home. Various Asian cultures first appeared in this recipe thousands of years ago, while Western influences are relatively new. Some ingredients have been added sparsely; others, like China, have dominated the dish. Still, no matter how foreign arrivals and interventions may have altered the salad's basic flavor, over centuries it remains unmistakably Vietnamese.

The people who are considered the ancestors of today's Vietnamese evolved from Indonesian, Mongolian Chinese, and Thai groups. They displaced the aboriginals of South Pacific origin who were living in the region. The native aboriginals were forced into the highlands where their descendants, a variety of sometimes warring clans, live there in relative isolation even today.

THE DONG SON CIVILIZATION

During the Bronze Age, from the thirteenth to the second centuries B.C., a thriving civilization developed at Dong Son, a district in the present-day northern province of Thanh Hoa. The Dongsonian culture reached from south of present-day Hanoi in the Red River Delta into central areas and first shaped the country, at that time called Van Lung. Its people were called Lac. They were ruled over by a succession of eighteen kings, called Hung. Today, the people of the Dong Son civilization, known as the Lac Viet, are considered by modern Vietnamese to be the first identifiable Vietnamese.

The Dong Son civilization survived comfortably as sailors, hunters, farmers, miners, and smelters. It also produced skilled artists who produced unique artifacts. Their art includes huge ornate bronze drums, known as rain drums, believed to have imitated thunder when beaten and so used magically to encourage and signal the appearance of rain. The exteriors of existing Dong Son drums display etched pictures of birds, hunts, and fishing boats, as well as tiny animal and human sculptures on their handles. In the second century B.C., however, the Chinese invaded the Red River Delta and the Dongsonian culture faded into history.

THE MARK OF INDIA

Vietnam's early history also bears the mark of another large neighbor, India. India influenced Vietnam historically through trade and culture. The Hindu religion, for instance, which is practiced today by some Vietnamese, comes from

Artists from the Dong Son civilization crafted bronze drums like this one, thought to have magical power.

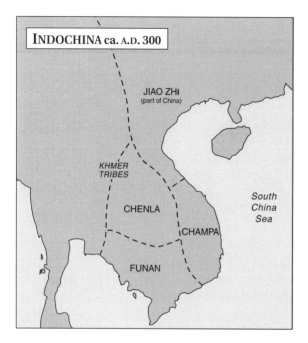

INDOCHINA ca. A.D. 300

JIAO ZHI
(part of China)

KHMER
TRIBES

CHENLA

CHAMPA

South
China
Sea

FUNAN

India. The rise and fall of two kingdoms in Vietnam is rooted in India's significant cultural influence. The Vietnamese kingdom of Funan existed in the southern region between the first and sixth centuries A.D. The Funan kingdom adopted the Hindu religion, Sanskrit writing and language, and Indian styles of art and architecture. Its people constructed elaborate canals and traded actively with other countries.

During the same period, in the second century A.D., the kingdom of Champa appeared in the central region. The Cham, too, traded with and were influenced by India.

The Chams' descendants still form a culturally identifiable ethnic minority living peacefully in central Vietnam, but the members of the Champa kingdom were once feared as an aggressive people, conducting sea raids against the shorelines of the Vietnamese to the north and their western neighbors, the Khmer, in what is now Cambodia. The Vietnamese army swept south and conquered the Champa kingdom in 1471. The Vietnamese destroyed the Cham capital and trading center of Indrapura, killing 40,000 of its residents in the process.

Ruins of Cham temples, huge sandstone friezes and sculptures of mythical sea monsters, religious figures such as the Hindu god Siva, and representations of real animals such as lions and elephants survive to remind us that the vanished Champa kingdom was once a great cultural center.

CHINA'S ENDURING INFLUENCE

Although Indian culture made its mark in the two kingdoms of Funan and Champa, neighboring China had the most enduring influence on Vietnam. For centuries, Vietnamese independence was continually threatened or lost to China. The constant struggle against this giant helped toughen the Vietnamese national character into the cohesive, militarily able force that proved strong enough to crush the Champa kingdom.

Much of China's influence was, in fact, positive. The Chinese introduced the practice of rice farming, which requires collective effort because the work requires many hands cooperating together in the rhythms of planting and harvest. As a result, Vietnamese villages became tightly bonded communities.

Each of these communities was autonomous. Councils of prominent local leaders selected by villagers governed individual villages. Though at various times emperors reigned over Vietnam, they were considered symbolic, divine connections between heaven and earth; as a Vietnamese adage says, "The edicts of the emperor stop at the edge of the village."[5]

According to journalist and historian Stanley Karnow, the more or less constant threat of foreign intrusion led villages to form "a unified chain of separate links to fight. Their country's frequent wars also infused in the Vietnamese a readiness to defend themselves, so that they evolved into a breed of warriors."[6]

Ruins of Cham temples (like this one dating back to the seventh century) still stand in Vietnam today.

★ THE TRUNG SISTERS

Trung Trac was a noblewoman whose husband, a dissident feudal lord, had been put to death by the Chinese. In A.D. 40, she joined her sister, Trung Nhi, to organize the other nobles and their underlings against the Chinese in the Hai Ba Trung Rebellion. Victorious, the sisters established themselves as queens in an independent country reaching north from Central Vietnam. Their reign proved short-lived, however, as the Chinese overpowered the Trung sisters two years later at the Battle of Lang-ba. The queens chose death over capture and jumped from a bridge to drown in the waters of the Hat Giang River.

Thousands of rebels were slain in that crucial battle. General Ma Yuan, the victor, did not let the sisters' suicide deter him from sending their heads back to the Chinese court. Marching southward, his armies beheaded or deported other Vietnamese to China, destroying all the Lac holdings.

The Trung sisters led an unsuccessful rebellion against the Chinese.

Invasions from China began in 208 B.C., when Chinese general Trieu Da conquered a section of the northern mountains of Vietnam and declared himself emperor of Nam Viet, or Land of the Southern Viet. Later, in A.D. 111, Nam Viet, which extended to the central area of the present nation, was seized by China and renamed Giao Chi Province. China's influence now became a force that would shape Vietnam's future for more than a thousand years. The Chinese appointed military governors to administer districts of the province.

Civilian advisers, an educated upper class known as mandarins, imported the teachings of the philosopher Confucius, whose ethical precepts were a vital part of Chinese culture. His teachings included obedience to authority and the importance of education. The Chinese established schools where Chinese was spoken and Confucian philosophy was taught.

The Chinese also exerted a positive influence when they introduced advances in technology. They built dikes and roads, introduced the plow and draft animals to upgrade agricultural practices, and contributed their knowledge of science and medical arts.

But the Chinese were still conquerors in Vietnam. China imposed high taxes, demanded troops and forced labor that amounted to slavery, took valuable goods such as pearls and ivory, and perhaps worst of all to the village-oriented Vietnamese, meddled in local matters of government.

REBELLIONS

In response, the Vietnamese rebelled against Chinese dominance. The first of ten major Vietnamese rebellions against the Chinese occurred in A.D. 42. Its two leaders, the Trung sisters, remain heroes to this day. Although ultimately beaten in battle by the Chinese, they ruled for two years.

After the defeat of the Trung sisters and the rebels who followed them, Chinese rule became more repressive and the Chinese insisted the Vietnamese adopt Chinese customs and clothing. The Vietnamese continued to resist Chinese sovereignty with periodic uprisings. Some of the rebels who rose up against the Chinese were native Chinese feudal lords who held power in Vietnam on lands granted them by Chinese rulers. These privileged nobles also wanted independence from China and began to see that their efforts would be stronger if peasants also joined them in throwing off Chinese rule. The seeds of Vietnamese nationalism were sown.

Despite continuous rebel activity, mighty China prevailed. By A.D. 679, the Chinese renamed the conquered land Annum, which means the Pacified South.

THE FIRST GUERRILLA TACTICS

The decisive Battle of the Bach Dang River, a northern waterway, took place in A.D. 938. It is historically significant not only for freeing Vietnam from the yoke of Chinese oppression, but also because it is the first recorded use by the Vietnamese of guerrilla warfare, those deceptive military tactics that would later prove so devastating to the French and the Americans.

Ngo Quyen ordered his men to drive iron-tipped spikes into the riverbed, hidden below the water's surface. When his troops engaged an expected arrival of armed Chinese junks, he retreated before low tide. As the Chinese chased his boats, their junks were impaled, and Ngo Quyen returned to defeat his trapped enemy.

INDEPENDENCE

A rebellion led by Ngo Quyen in A.D. 938 against a weakened Chinese Tang dynasty finally resulted in Vietnamese independence. In 967, Ngo's descendant Dinh Bo Linh became emperor, calling his kingdom Dai Co Viet, the Kingdom of the Watchful Hawk. The practical leader of a largely peasant army whose officers were intellectuals, he made a temporary peace with China.

Although Vietnam's independence would be short-lived, during the Ly dynasty that followed the brief rule of Dinh Bo Linh, the country enjoyed a period of prosperity which included a reorganization of government, the founding of the nation's first university, the Temple of Literature, in 1070, and initial public works projects aimed at controlling floodwaters.

In 1287, the Vietnamese pushed back the fierce Mongol emperor Kublai Khan in a battle in the Red River Valley. The khan and his army had thundered south from China, hungry for control of Indonesian trade routes, but three hundred thousand Mongols proved no match for the guerrilla battle tactics of the Vietnamese.

Strong and independent after driving out the Mongols, the militarily sophisticated and savvy Vietnamese destroyed the Champa kingdom and expanded south.

RETURN OF THE GIANT

Although battle hardened, the Vietnamese were also battle weary after fighting the Mongols and the Cham. China was under the control of a powerful new dynasty, the Ming, which crushed the Vietnamese in 1407.

As conqueror, China threatened to extinguish Vietnamese culture. Vietnamese literature was seized and all education from that time on was conducted in Chinese. Women had to wear Chinese fashions; men were forbidden to cut their hair and forced to adopt the long braid or queue in the Chinese style. Peasants became slaves, forced to labor in mines, forests, and spice fields. Tax collection reached new heights of efficiency with each Vietnamese family issued an identification card to aid in revenue retrieval and control by the Chinese.

General Tran Hung Dao (center) used guerrilla tactics to defeat the Mongol army in the thirteenth century.

MORE REBELLION

Such harsh measures bred yet another rebellion by the Vietnamese. Le Loi, who led the rebellion, was the son of a prosperous landowning family and had earned a reputation among the poor for his generosity. In 1410 Le Loi began gathering an army of peasants, workers, even petty criminals, and began training them in remote mountain camps to be guerrilla fighters against the Chinese.

In a departure from the usual military practice in wartime, Le Loi's guerrilla army did not force local farmers to feed them. Instead, Le Loi persuaded the people to see the political and moral rightness of the cause for which his army struggled. He tried first to capture the people's hearts so that they would willingly support and fight alongside him. Le Loi's creed is summed up in his own words: "Every man on earth ought to accomplish some great enterprise so that he leaves the sweetness of his name to later generations. How then, could he willingly be the slave of foreigners?"[7]

The Chinese tried to protect themselves from the guerrilla army by building towers on the roads to watch over their troops. In the end, that did not help. Le Loi, finally backed by strength in numbers, attacked the horse cavalry of the Chinese, with his own soldiers riding war elephants. He won the decisive battle in 1426 in a field near present-day Hanoi, which he then made his capital, calling the city Dong Kinh.

A GOLDEN AGE

In the fifteenth century, Vietnam enjoyed a cultural renaissance that combined Confucian principles imported by the Chinese and native Vietnamese customs and traditions. Chinese influences had by now been infused into Vietnamese consciousness, and Confucian ethics, which emphasized the importance of education and respect for authority, prevailed in social and political life.

Emperor Le Thanh Tong modeled his government along Confucian lines. Power passed downward from a series of ministries, departments, headquarters, and district offices to eight thousand communes, each with its own mayor. This type of organization established a firm central authority, while still allowing for the local flexibility so prized by the peasants. The emperor received great respect, but his power still stopped at the village gate.

As emperor, Le Thanh Tong sponsored educational reform and encouraged pride in all things Vietnamese. He used a national census and a draft to create a huge standing army. In keeping with the prevailing emphasis on scholarship, army officers achieved their positions by taking competitive examinations. Le Thanh Tong was an avid scholar himself, and expanded the university. Under his rule, the Vietnamese language was restored in the educational system. Poetry and anthologies of Vietnamese legends reappeared, and mathematical and scientific treatises, including the first complete map of Vietnam, were produced.

Legal reforms under the emperor led to a liberal code of law that protected citizens against abuse by elite mandarins, who were upper-class government officials, and gave women nearly equal rights with men. In keeping with Confucianism, however, threats to authority brought severe punishment. For example, a student who disobeyed a teacher could be exiled, and slaves could be put to death for showing a lack of respect to their owners.

The ideas and principles of Confucius became popular in Vietnam during the fifteenth century.

CIVIL STRIFE

Le Thanh Tong's heirs ruled until 1788, but uneasily and with little actual power. Various clans competed and schemed for the real power. By the early 1500s, the Le emperors had become mere figureheads while clans led by the Trinh family in the North and the Nguyen family in Central and South Vietnam battled for actual control.

By 1613 the two families had divided Vietnam into North and South, roughly at the 17th parallel. After two centuries of fighting, the families had finally reached a truce. But each secretly hoped to gain strength and eventually defeat the other and rule over both North and South. This longstanding distrust between the northern and southern regions festered and would make the reestablishment of a unified nation difficult for centuries to come. Still, the long struggle against China had implanted the notion of national identity firmly in Vietnamese hearts, both North and South.

3

FOREIGN DOMINATION AND INDEPENDENCE

China and India were not the only empires interested in Vietnam. Western powers of the European Renaissance, eager to trade for pepper, spices, gems, and textiles, likewise made inroads into Vietnam more than five hundred years ago. In the 1400s, bold Portuguese sailors established a settlement at what is now Danang. The Portuguese merchants, however, like the Dutch and English who followed, failed to flourish there because the Vietnamese were not at all receptive to foreign contact.

But Catholic Jesuit priests arrived along with the merchants, and where commerce failed, religion made lasting inroads. Vietnamese peasants welcomed Christianity's focus on individual importance and salvation, and, consequently, Vietnamese Catholic priests often became village leaders.

In 1627, Alexandre de Rhodes, a linguist and French Jesuit priest, developed quoc ngu, a script that used the Roman alphabet for written Vietnamese. Because the Roman alphabet was much simpler than Chinese script, its broad use made the Christian Gospel more accessible to the people.

The upper-class mandarins, who held their high public administrative positions through the authority of the rigid Chinese Confucian system, feared that Western religious thought, with its emphasis on the individual, might weaken their power. The Vietnamese emperors showed less concern. Although wary of Westerners, they included Jesuit scholars in their courts for their knowledge of Western medicine, astronomy, and mathematics, as well as for their connections to European arms suppliers.

In the eighteenth century, internal unrest surged in Vietnam, due partly to peasants' resentment against unfair taxation. The powerful Nguyen family was deposed during the Tay Son Rebellion of 1772, started by three wealthy brothers who found popular support among peasants tired of repressive treatment at the hands of mandarins. Three years later, the insurgents captured Saigon (present-day Ho Chi Minh City), killing 10,000 Chinese residents in the process. The Tay Son then moved north, finally unifying Vietnam.

In response, the deposed Nguyen Anh took the first steps that ultimately made Vietnam vulnerable to French takeover. He sent his four-year-old son, Canh, along with a French bishop, to the court of Louis XVI to petition the king to intercede on Nguyen Anh's behalf so that he could regain the throne. The beautiful Asian child and his exotic entourage caused a sensation at the fashion-conscious court. Although Louis XVI backed out of an agreement to mobilize French troops to fight in Vietnam, French merchants privately funded French fighters who fought with Nguyen soldiers to defeat the Tay Son in 1799. The winning army's leader was Canh, now grown.

French influence in Vietnam began during the eighteenth century when Louis XVI sent troops to quash the Tay Son Rebellion.

In 1802 the victorious Nguyen Anh, self-crowned emperor, adopted the title of Gia Long, and built his capital at Hue. There he constructed the famed Citadel, his castle-fortress. He rebuilt his war-torn country's roads and bridges, but in the process burdened his people with heavy taxes and used peasants as forced labor, which naturally created popular resentment.

Trouble was compounded by the next Nguyen emperor, who distrusted Westerners, thinking them barbaric. After ascending the throne, Gia Long's son, Ming Mang, ordered the execution of several priests and many Vietnamese Catholics. Then his successor imprisoned and deported foreign missionaries. This angered France, which then established a fleet in Asian waters to protect French missionaries as well as business interests.

FRENCH OCCUPATION

France's move for control of Vietnam began in 1858, when a French armada of fourteen vessels and twenty-five hundred men launched a campaign to take the port of Tourane. They reasoned that Vietnam should give up Tourane to compensate France for the bad treatment of French missionaries. In terms of defense, what the Vietnamese could not do alone, heat, humidity, and disease did for them. Typhoid, malaria, dysentery, and tuberculosis, as well as cholera and unknown fevers, ravaged the French, who waited in vain for support from Vietnamese Catholics as the troops languished and grew weaker on their ships. Many more soldiers died from disease than battle. Before giving up and leaving in the face of increasingly aggressive Vietnamese opposition, the French commander Rigault de Genouilly wrote, "Everything here tends toward ruin."[8]

But the French returned, and successfully took Saigon in 1861. Beset, the Vietnamese emperor Tu Duc doubted his ability to beat back French aggression, and to save his monarchy, decreed southern Vietnam to be a French protectorate. As a protectorate, southern Vietnam would fall under the partial control of France. An annual tribute, trade rights, and French occupation of Saigon and surrounding provinces were part of the bargain.

France described its actions as a *mission civilisatrice*, which meant the French would bring their culture and reli-

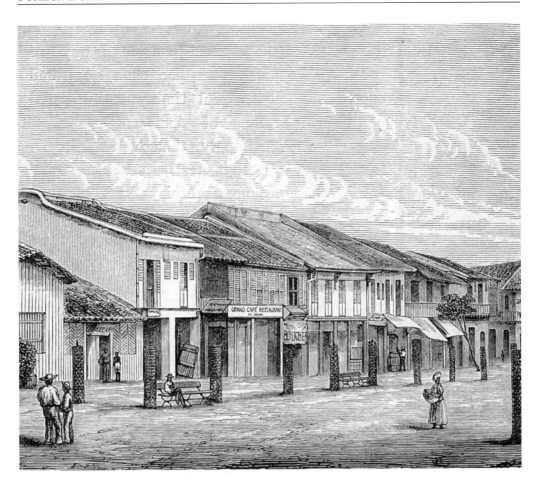

gion to the Vietnamese, whom they perceived as unfortunate heathens. To further its colonial rule, France launched naval expeditions on the Mekong and Red Rivers.

When Saigon (shown here) was captured by the French in 1861, the Vietnamese emperor admitted defeat and declared South Vietnam a French protectorate.

Although they met with resistance, by 1874 the French had sufficiently overpowered the Vietnamese that Emperor Tu Duc agreed to French entry into the northern regions. The French had long been hungry to mine rich anthracite coal deposits there. Mineral resources, as well as lucrative trade and the development of tea, coffee, and rubber plantations had fueled France's keen interest in Vietnam.

While labeled a protectorate, Vietnam had actually become a French possession, or colony. By 1883, France ruled all three regions of Vietnam. Instead of one nation known as Vietnam, the French established three administrative zones: Tonkin, in the North; Annam, in the Central region, and

Cochinchina, in the South. All Vietnamese were now called Annamites.

Like the harsh dynasties before them, the French imposed heavy taxes. Only a small population of wealthy Vietnamese kept large tracts of land. Most Vietnamese peasants lost their lands and became sharecroppers or indentured workers. At times, peasants were allowed to keep only one bag of rice for every eleven harvested, which meant that some people were literally taxed to death by starvation. When renters failed to pay, landlords could turn the renters out, beat, or even kill them.

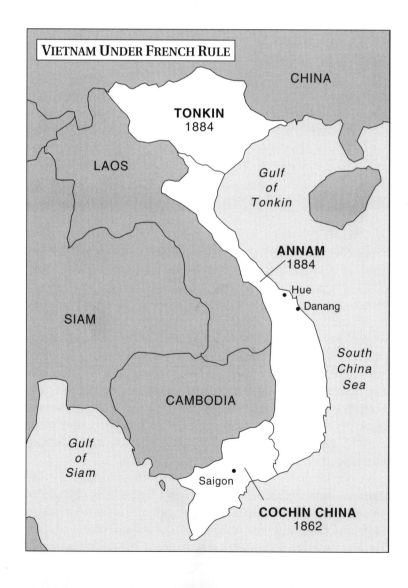

VIETNAM UNDER FRENCH RULE

Out of necessity, indentured servants often agreed to work on large tea, rubber, or coffee plantations; as laborers on railroads; or in the anthracite, tungsten, coal, tin, or zinc mines for subsistence wages. Thousands died of disease and malnutrition.

When the French colonized Vietnam, the literacy rate stood at 80 percent. Seventy years later, only 5 percent of Vietnamese could read. Schools were not provided for the impoverished peasants, although some taught their children to write with bamboo slivers on the backs of banana leaves, the veins serving as guidelines. Upper-class Vietnamese children did receive an education in French-run schools and were sometimes sent to Paris to complete their studies. Often, though, they returned to Vietnam to find that their training exceeded professional opportunities available to natives.

One of the most destructive French innovations in Vietnam was a quick-burning type of opium, a highly addictive drug derived from poppies. The sale of opium in Asian and European markets proved highly profitable for the French. It was devastating for the Vietnamese, however, many of whom resorted to opium as a way to numb the pain of poverty, hunger, and despair.

THE RESISTANCE

Throughout the colonial period, Vietnamese resistance to the French continued. From 1859 until the French were beaten in 1954, guerrilla fighters hid in swamps and marshes like the Plain of Reeds, using hit-and-run tactics: appearing—disappearing—confusing and frustrating the French troops. Aristocrats and peasants alike sacrificed their lives willingly for a Vietnam free of foreign domination.

The French responded to this resistance by beheading rebels on the guillotine, torturing prisoners, burning any villages that provided cover for dissidents, and killing the leaders of such villages. Major unsuccessful Vietnamese uprisings in 1930 and again in 1940 brought harsh reprisals from the French.

It was during this time that Ho Chi Minh, Vietnam's revolutionary leader, began his life's work. At first, Minh's focus was on nationhood for a unified Vietnam. But when no democratic Western country showed interest in his cause, he sought allies in communist countries and adopted the communist

HO CHI MINH

Ho Chi Minh is revered by most Vietnamese as the father of their nation, unified and independent at last. He was born Nguyen Sinh Cung in 1890 in Hue, where his father was a government official and teacher. Like many Vietnamese, Ho grew up hearing poetry and stories of his people's struggle for independence from foreign domination.

Although educated at a French school in Hue, Ho hated French colonial rule and in 1911 left Vietnam to work his way around the world. He saw Boston and San Francisco and worked in the navy yards of Brooklyn and a restaurant kitchen in New York. He was an assistant pastry chef in London and a portrait photographer in Paris, where he mingled with intellectuals and the many Vietnamese living there.

Then he joined the French Communist Party and wrote leftist articles. Slight and shy, he did not appear to be a political firebrand, but he had an absolute dedication to a free Vietnam. In Paris he took the name Nguyen Ai Quoc, which means Nguyen the Patriot.

For thirty years he traveled, studied, organized communist groups and Vietnamese expatriots, and spent time in and out of prison. He escaped from a prison in Hong Kong, taking many aliases after that. And he wrote. He would write poetry and political tracts all his life.

When World War II brought Japanese forces to Vietnam, Ho slipped back into the country even though he suffered the debilitating effects of tuberculosis and malaria. He joined the resistance and took his final alias, Ho Chi Minh, Bringer of Light. His fellow revolutionaries called him Bac Ho, Uncle Ho.

When elected president of North Vietnam in 1945, he declined to live in the presidential palace in Hanoi. Instead, he lived in a simple house behind it.

He died of heart failure on September 2, 1969. Although he did not live to see a unified Vietnam, Ho Chi Minh inspired people during his life and after his death to make his dream a reality.

Ho Chi Minh, the father of Vietnam.

philosophy. To him, the idea of a classless society, with collective ownership of property under the firm control of a one-party government, seemed the answer to Vietnam's problems.

WORLD WAR II

World War II disrupted Vietnam's struggle for independence from France, and brought new suffering to the nation. The French drafted Vietnamese to be soldiers, and when France fell to Nazi Germany, Japanese troops, allies of the Nazis, occupied Vietnam. At first, the Vietnamese welcomed the Japanese, but the Japanese took nearly all the rice crops and forced the Vietnamese to grow inedible crops, such as jute, to provide rope for Japan's war efforts. Terrible poverty and famine resulted, and by 1945, one person in six had died of starvation or disease.

During the war, the Vietnamese were without matches, lamp oil, or even cloth. In her book *After Sorrow*, American author Lady Borton quotes a Vietnamese friend who remembers:

> It was embarrassing to have no cloth. Imagine! We made clothes out of leaves and stitched them with banana thread! A husband and wife might own a single pair of shorts. When the wife wore the shorts outside the house, the husband hid inside.[9]

While WWII was raging, Ho Chi Minh established the League for the Independence of Vietnam, later to be known as the Vietminh. The league comprised Vietnamese of all ages and social classes who resisted Japanese occupation. Led by communists, many of the Vietminh hid in the mountains and helped to rescue American fighter pilots downed by the Japanese during missions to deliver supplies to China. In turn, for the league's help, Ho Chi Minh received weapons and aid from both America and China. By the war's end, the Vietminh controlled North Vietnam.

HO CHI MINH DECLARES INDEPENDENCE

On August 16, 1945, Ho Chi Minh declared himself president of a provisional government of Vietnam known as the National Liberation Committee. Emperor Bao Dai resigned, handing power over to the Vietminh. On September 2, 1945, Ho Chi Minh publicly declared the formation of the independent

Ho Chi Minh (shown here) brought communism to Southeast Asia.

nation of the Democratic Republic of Vietnam. His words included passages drawn from America's own Declaration of Independence: "We hold the truth that all men are created equal . . . endowed with certain inalienable rights, among them life, liberty, and the pursuit of happiness."[10]

Ho Chi Minh hoped for American support against French efforts to maintain colonial rule, but that support did not materialize. Ho Chi Minh wrote letter after letter to President Harry S. Truman asking that America recognize Vietnam as an independent nation. Mindful of how strong an ally France had been during WWII, Truman never replied.

A nonviolent coexistence between Vietminh troops and France endured until 1946, when the French fired on Vietminh in the port of Haiphong in festering disputes over collection of customs duties. The war with France had begun.

WAR WITH FRANCE

On one side were the French and some of the upper-class Vietnamese, mainly Catholic, who shared religious and anticommunist sympathies with France. On the other side were the Vietminh and some of the country's noncommunist nationals.

The major world powers sided with their ideological allies. Communist China and the Soviet Union supported the Vietminh cause. The United States committed itself to providing aid to France.

Despite eight years of fighting and $2.5 billion in aid from America, France could not defeat the Vietminh. When the French lost the fifty-seven-day battle known as the siege of Dien Bien Phu in 1954, the war ended.

Meeting in Switzerland two and a half months later, in late July, the French and Vietnamese reached an agreement known as the Geneva Accords. Vietnam was partitioned for a second time at the 17th parallel, dividing it into the Democratic Republic of Vietnam (the North) and the Republic of Vietnam (the South). The Vietminh stayed or regrouped in the North, claiming Hanoi as their capital. The French and pro-French Vietnamese stayed in, or moved to, the South,

The Vietnamese war with France ended in 1954 with the fall of Dien Bien Phu.

whose capital was Saigon. The agreement provided for only a temporary division of Vietnam with national elections scheduled for 1956.

A NATION DIVIDED

After Vietnam's division, life in both the North and the South demanded that the people adapt to very different governments. Likewise, the leaders of these new governments faced different challenges.

Leadership in the South went to Ngo Dinh Diem, a strong anticommunist from a Catholic family of Central Vietnam. The United States, whose goal was to establish a democratic Vietnam, supplied Diem with both money and military advisers.

General Delteil of France signed a peace accord officially ending the war between France and Vietnam.

THE STRATEGIC HAMLETS PROGRAM

South Vietnamese peasants found themselves facing new cruelties when Ngo Dinh, Diem's younger brother, ran the secret police and the strategic hamlets program, a counterinsurgency plan supported by President John F. Kennedy. By the strategic hamlets program, peasants were forced to leave their homes and live in barbed-wire compounds, supposedly to keep them safe from, but in reality to stop them from helping the NLF. This program and later programs that relocated villagers into cities were public relations disasters. Peasants were uprooted from their ancient home villages and from the graves of their revered ancestors, inciting many outraged Vietnamese to join, or at least support, the Viet Cong.

Diem was a staunch Catholic and some 900,000 Catholic refugees fleeing the North strengthened his position in the largely Buddhist South. A bachelor, Diem made his brother's Catholic wife, Madame Nhu, first lady of Vietnam. Although she tried to identify herself as the reincarnation of the Trung sisters, her hatred of the Buddhists, who did not support Diem, and her encouragement of repressive measures against them made her unpopular.

Buddhist activists began a series of public protests following an incident in Hue in 1963 when police opened fire on a peaceful gathering intended to celebrate the birthday of Buddha. Diem imposed martial law, the use of military troops to enforce order.

Realizing that he could not win a national election over the more popular Ho Chi Minh, Diem refused to allow the planned nationwide elections to take place. Instead, he declared himself president of South Vietnam and his regime was recognized internationally by many anticommunist nations.

Diem's refusal to honor the Geneva Accords infuriated many Vietnamese. His favoritism for Catholics, promoting them to positions in government and the military, and his failure to continue land reform programs accomplished by the Vietminh, who had given back sections of land to the peasants, led to increasing guerrilla insurgency. Buddhist monks and nuns burned themselves alive in public demonstrations. University students protested against Diem. Anti-Diem forces including gangsters, Buddhist leaders, and communists hid out in the Mekong Delta.

Diem was ultimately overthrown in a military coup; he was assassinated on November 2, 1963. His successors, President Nguyen Van Thieu and Vice President Nguyen Cao Ky proved equally unpopular. During their time in power, government corruption and inefficiency continued.

As repressive as Diem's policies were, life in the North was at times even harsher. Ho Chi Minh's communist government resorted to brutality in its efforts to impose control. Landowners, even those with very small plots, were killed by teams of cadres, or communist leaders, appointed to agricultural reform tribunals. Quotas were established for the execution of alleged French sympathizers, former landowners, and people deemed insufficiently enthusiastic in their support of the Vietminh. Thousands of people were put to death or imprisoned in the early years of Ho Chi Minh's regime.

Buddhist monks and nuns burned themselves alive in public demonstrations protesting Diem's staunch Catholic government.

In 1960 the government in Hanoi announced formation of the National Liberation Front in the South. The NLF called for the solidification of various factions in Vietnam, for withdrawal of all foreign troops, and for reunification. The NLF were dubbed Viet Cong by South Vietnam's government, a slang term for Vietnamese communist.

President Thieu (shown here) succeeded Diem and proved to be equally unpopular.

THE VIETNAM WAR

By this time, American involvement in Vietnam had grown well beyond contributing to France's effort to maintain colonial control over Vietnam. About fifteen thousand American military personnel were in Vietnam. The United States was providing expertise, training, and equipment to the South Vietnamese army, and had given $500 million in aid to South Vietnam in 1963.

America's increased presence in Vietnam resulted largely from fear that communism, once established in Vietnam, would take hold in other countries throughout Southeast Asia. American leaders believed this would threaten America's long-term financial interests in the region as well as hurt

THE TUNNELS OF CU CHI

Poorly equipped Vietnamese guerrillas began using tunnels with openings disguised or protected by foliage to protect themselves from enemy bombs and heavy artillery during their war with France in the late 1940s.

The hard red dirt of the Cu Chi district, now part of Ho Chi Minh City, allowed for an elaborate tunnel system more than two hundred miles long at its completion in the 1960s. Viet Cong dug some tunnels several stories deep, with large rooms designated for soldiers' rest and recreation, hospitals, warehouses, weapons factories, and kitchens.

The Viet Cong developed secure communication systems via the tunnels and a relatively safe means of slipping into Saigon, the South Vietnamese capital. They could execute surprise attacks from the tunnels and vanish back into them without a trace. The surprise attacks on Saigon during the 1968 Tet Offensive originated from the tunnels of Cu Chi. Sections of the Cu Chi tunnel system even ran beneath an American army base.

When ground attacks against the tunnels resulted in heavy casualties, Americans dropped bombs and defoliants on Cu Chi. Still, the labyrinthine tunnels stayed useful to the Viet Cong.

Vietnamese guerrillas used tunnels (like these in Saigon) to elude French and American soldiers.

chances for building new alliances with other democratically run governments.

On August 4, 1964, a U.S. destroyer conducting surveillance in the Gulf of Tonkin, the *Maddox*, clashed with North Vietnamese patrol boats. North Vietnam claimed the *Maddox* was inside the limits of international waters, which meant it was unlawfully invading North Vietnamese–controlled seas. President Lyndon Johnson, frustrated by the fact that American military were only allowed to act in an advisory capacity to South Vietnamese troops, saw the incident as an opportunity to justify escalation of American military activity in the area.

When the *Maddox* and another U.S. ship returned to the scene, radar picked up what may have been torpedoes launched against them. Johnson asked Congress to pass a resolution giving him the power to "take all necessary measures to repel attacks against the U.S." and "prevent further aggression" as well as to "determine when peace and security in the area had been attained."[11]

When the resolution passed, Johnson sent the first U.S. military combat troops to join the Army of the Republic of Vietnam, or ARVN. U.S. Marines disembarked at Danang in Central Vietnam in March 1965. The first major battle of the Vietnam War took place that year near Laos in the jungle-covered La Drang Valley.

The ensuing civil war was long and costly. By the time the last American troops departed from Vietnam in 1973 the death toll on all sides was enormous. At war's end, 440,000 communists, 223,748 ARVN, 4,000,000 civilians, and 58,183 Americans had died. The extent of psychological and physical wounds is impossible to gauge.

Financial losses, however, easily reached into the billions. The financial cost to the United States alone was $150 billion. However it is figured, the war devastated both North and South Vietnam. Mountainous and plains areas were ravaged. The infrastructure in the North lay in ruins, with major cities bombed nearly to rubble. The South was also bombed and suffered the most damage to its farmland because of the application of millions of gallons of defoliants such as Agent Orange. Some sixteen hundred irrigation systems were damaged. Of South Vietnamese villages, some were rebuilt only to be bombed again; in all, nine thousand of fifteen thousand were destroyed.

THE SEIGE OF KHE SANH AND THE TET OFFENSIVE

With U.S. military strength and technology unable to defeat the Viet Cong's nationalism and guerrilla tactics, the Vietnam War had no foreseeable end. However, in January 1968, two offensive actions, the siege of Khe Sanh and the Tet Offensive, changed the course of war.

The seige of Khe Sanh, a U.S. Marine base, lasted 77 days. The marines held the position but suffered eighteen hundred casualties; the communists lost ten thousand. Then, on January 30, 1968, nearly seventy thousand communist troops entered more than one hundred cities and towns including Saigon, where they captured, and for a few hours held, the U.S. embassy. The Tet Offensive, which lasted until February 25, was a military disaster for the communists, who sustained heavy casualties and failed to realize expected support from the people.

President Lyndon Johnson halted American bombing in responce to public antiwar sentiment following televised coverage of U.S. bombing of cities such as Hue in South Vietnam during the Tet Offensive. Public support for American involvement in Vietnam decreased from that point on.

Refugees flee Tet fighting in 1968.

AMERICAN WITHDRAWAL

The Vietnam War ended on January 27, 1973, with the signing of the Paris Peace Agreement. Two years later, on April 29, 1975, the last Americans departed from Saigon. Thousands of South Vietnamese who had sided with the Americans, now fearing the takeover by the communists of the North, hysterically fought to be included on buses and helicopters evacuating the area. On April 30, 1975, communist forces entered Saigon.

After decades of struggle, Vietnam was a unified nation free of foreign domination or intervention. The price paid in lives lost and disrupted, and an urban and rural landscape despoiled by warfare, was high. The surviving people of Vietnam stood poised on the brink of a new epoch in their nation's turbulent history.

The signing of the Paris Peace Agreement ended the Vietnam War.

4

AN ECONOMY
IN TRANSITION

When the communists took over South Vietnam in 1976, they inherited potentially productive land and factories, but they did not inherit a healthy economy. The formerly capitalist South had come to rely on American financial aid to cover its budget deficit and to keep its commercial economy flowing

The Vietnam War left the South in ruins.

with goods and services. America had supplied the money for the training of South Vietnam's military and police forces. Further, the Americans in Vietnam spent freely, flooding the market with cash, and Vietnamese entrepreneurs raised prices to profit from their relatively rich visitors. Ordinary Vietnamese could not afford to pay what Americans could and did spend on goods and services. As a result, inflation was rampant. Without American money, the economy slowed and the demand for consumer goods diminished.

Moreover, South Vietnamese business owners had stopped making long-term investments out of fear of a communist takeover. Landowners, who traditionally had more money than the average citizen, either hoarded their cash or spent it all on luxury goods in fear that their money would become worthless in a postwar economy.

The infrastructure—housing, transportation, and communications networks in both urban and rural areas in the North and South—had been devastated. The task of reorganizing and rebuilding could only be described as massive. Seven million tons of bombs had been dropped on Vietnam during the war, leaving 20 million bomb craters and sweeping areas destroyed by bombs and toxic chemicals like Agent Orange. Thousands of South Vietnamese villages were ruined. Every bridge in North Vietnam had been bombed and hundreds of irrigation systems damaged. Many of the people between the ages of twenty and forty, particularly men, were dead. More carried mental and physical scars from the war. Malnutrition continued to be a problem. Jobs had disappeared and education had been disrupted. Opium addiction, prostitution, and crime were widespread.

COMMUNIST CONTROL

All of this complicated the already complex transition to a unified communist Vietnam. The communist government maintained firm control and permitted little personal freedom, managing virtually every aspect of life. The people technically owned all land and industry collectively, but only under the firm leadership of the Communist Party. Cadres,

After the communist takeover, all private industry (including rice paddies like these) were put under government control.

leaders in the Communist Party, controlled virtually all agencies and organizations, including the communal agricultural units known as collectives.

At first, after the communist takeover, a provisional revolutionary government made up of southerners who had been members of the National Liberation Front but not necessarily communist, filled government positions. In short order, however, the government in Hanoi took full control over events in the South.

Evidence of communist dominance could be seen in the July 1976 national election, in which only communist-approved candidates appeared on the ballot and people who did not vote lost their food ration cards. Distrust worsened when the government in Hanoi, now the country's capital, sent cadres from the North to run offices and agencies. Southerners who had supported the Viet Cong especially resented the lack of recognition for their efforts during the war.

Society entered a period of new turbulence after the communist takeover. The cities of the South faced urgent problems needing immediate solutions, from garbage collection to high rates of drug addiction and prostitution. In the years before the war's end, thousands of peasants had relocated as refugees to urban centers, and now at least a million former members of the armed services and police, as well as former South Vietnamese civil servants, were newly unemployed.

Adding to these problems, the new government freed all prisoners from South Vietnamese jails under the assumption that they had been imprisoned because they were procommunist. This, however, raised street crime rates as newly released criminals returned to their former ways of life. The prisons were refilled with political opponents, including former members of the ARVN, those who had worked for or cooperated with the Americans, or those simply not deemed dedicated to communism.

Poverty grew with the sudden change in currency. When the South Vietnamese piastre was replaced by the North Vietnamese dong, many people awoke to find themselves suddenly destitute. Business owners lost their means of livelihood. Within six months all private industry, including transportation and farm collectives, was put under the central control of the government, which set quotas for production.

THE NEW ECONOMIC ZONES

Nearly as destabilizing as reeducation camps were areas designated New Economic Zones, or NEZs. In addition to other problems, the government faced nearly unmanageable postwar population growth. It tried to relocate people by the millions from North Vietnam and the coastal regions to NEZs in the less populated Central Highlands or the Mekong Delta. These tended to be uncultivated areas with poor soil, harsh living conditions, and no infrastructure. Failure far outweighed success in these settlements. Dislocated people tended to drift back to cities to live homeless on the streets.

Hundreds of thousands of former civil servants, army officers, doctors, lawyers, teachers, journalists, and other intellectuals were forced to enter reeducation centers or camps, sometimes called the Bamboo Gulag, where they were indoctrinated into communist ideology and every action was strictly controlled. Inmates attended indoctrination sessions on the evils of American imperialism and the victories of communists, took part in discussion groups, and were required to write essays about the lectures they were given. They were also forced to labor: digging wells, building fences, cutting trees, and clearing jungles.

The detainees at these reeducation camps were malnourished and many died of disease such as malaria. Those who resisted the indoctrination, or who were caught trying to escape, were sometimes tortured. Collected evidence from witnesses indicates as many as sixty-five thousand people, many in the camps, were executed for political reasons by the communists in the years following the reunification of Vietnam.

THE BOAT PEOPLE

In response to the dramatic changes brought by the communist takeover, many Vietnamese fled the country without official permission to enter new homelands. A stream of refugees, known as boat people because they left by sea, formed an exodus that began in 1975 and continued until the mid-1990s. It has been estimated that hundreds of thousands of people desperate to escape persecution or find a better economic future fled Vietnam. Many of these boat people perished at sea because of unsafe boats that capsized in shark-filled waters, shortages of food and drinking water, or at the hands of pirates who raped, robbed, and murdered them.

The boat people left in waves. The first, in 1975, were educated people, often connected to the military, who had access to boats and planes. The second were fishermen or other coastal people with boats. Then, starting in 1978 when relations soured between Vietnam and China, ethnic Chinese were expelled from Vietnam in numbers estimated to be as high as four hundred thousand. They were forced to forfeit their possessions and pay a heavy tax, about $2,000, before departing. Government officials often towed them out to the open sea in overcrowded, unsafe boats, leaving them to the mercy of pirates and the weather. Many died there, and many thousands of others still live in refugee camps in Indonesia, although many have also immigrated to Canada, the United States, and other countries. The Hong Kong government has attempted to repatriate, or send back, some of the refugees crowded into camps there. Some have returned, been

THE FINAL WAVE

The last wave of Vietnamese refugees since the late 1980s consisted of those involved in the Orderly Departure Program (ODP) carried out under the auspices of the United Nations High Commission for Refugees (UNHCR). The ODP was designed to provide safe evacuation and resettlement of refugees from Vietnam. Its primary goal was to reunite families and improve lives for Amerasian children fathered by American soldiers during the war. Such offspring are not well accepted by the rest of Vietnamese society. They often struggle to survive on the streets. When the program was turned over to the International Organization of Migration in 1991, 330,000 people had immigrated legally and safely.

A UNHCR screening process is now in place intended to distinguish those classed as refugees, who are escaping political persecution, from migrants seeking a better economic life outside Vietnam, sometimes because of employment layoffs resulting from economic reforms of formerly state-run industries, now undergoing privatization under *doi moi*.

granted a small allowance for resettlement, and been re-stored to Vietnamese citizenship.

Another group of refugees, the land people, tried to make it through Cambodia to Thailand, a perilous journey because of the murderous Khmer Rouge, or Cambodian communist forces under the harsh Cambodian ruler Pol Pot.

FOREIGN RELATIONS

Diplomatically, the young nation struggled as well. In the three years following the withdrawal of U.S. forces, rela-tions with the United States continued to be strained be-cause the Vietnamese insisted on war reparations in the amount of $3.5 billion, which they said had been promised by U.S. president Richard Nixon. The Vietnamese govern-ment had figured the amount into their economic plans. The United States, however, would not pay in part because of delays in delivery of the remains of U.S. soldiers listed as missing in action and the much-publicized plight of the boat people.

Vietnam's international relations were further frustrated after it invaded Cambodia in 1978. As a result of the invasion, China cut off aid. Peasants remember 1980 as one of their hungriest years.

Vietnam's relations with China hovered between outright hostility and frigid distance until Vietnam finally withdrew its troops from Cambodia in 1989. At first, China not only withheld aid, but also reacted to the invasion of their ally Cambodia by invading North Vietnam. Although the fighting only lasted 17 days, the Chinese troop withdrawal followed a scorched-earth policy, and crops and houses were de-stroyed in the process.

After China severed all trade relations following the Cam-bodian invasion, Vietnam's government turned to the Soviet Union for economic aid. The Soviet Union provided aid un-til its breakup in 1991. Cash-poor Vietnam paid back the So-viet Union under a barter system in which Vietnam traded agricultural products and resources such as sugar cane, rub-ber, crude oil, and wood for refined oil, machinery, and weapons from the Soviet Union. But unrefined products were less valuable than finished products, so the Soviet Union kept lending money and Vietnam's debt grew. By 1989, Vietnam owed $5.5 billion to the Soviet Union.

The Change to *Doi Moi*

Not even large amounts of Soviet aid could stem the coming economic collapse. By the 1980s, it became clear that Vietnam's rigid, Marxist style of communism had failed. According to an economic theory called the law of supply and demand, for an economy to succeed, the demand for goods and services must exceed, or at least equal, their supply. In Vietnam, production was low in both industry and agriculture because there was no profit incentive to get people to achieve good results in either manufacturing or farming efforts. Farmers' crops went for low prices to government collectors. Sugar cane growers found that central management had even set pricing costs below cost of production. That meant that even if harvests were good, there was no profit. With no personal incentive, workers' performance hit bottom, a major problem in a country that has traditionally held a strong work ethic.

Vietnamese industries were losing large amounts of money by the 1980s.

Because government policy did not conform to the law of supply and demand, production quotas of goods and con-

Nguyen Van Lihn reintroduced free enterprise and lessened the government's hold on the marketplace.

sumer needs simply did not match. Warehouses sat full of goods. Lacking technological knowledge for the production of high quality, saleable goods, industry failed because no one wanted the poor-quality products that were manufactured. Inflation of the dong, or Vietnamese unit of currency, stood at 800 to 1000 percent a year; thus, money was nearly worthless. Bad weather increased production problems and the economy further suffered because the United States and other democratic countries refused to trade with Vietnam.

The government realized a change was necessary. Three top leaders resigned and a dozen top ministers were fired. Nguyen Van Lihn, a progressive politician, became the new general secretary of the Vietnamese Communist Party.

Under his leadership, the Communist Party Central Committee reintroduced the profit incentive under a policy called *doi moi*, or renovation. *Doi moi* allowed for some forms of free enterprise and lessened state control in the marketplace. Since the implementation of this new approach, the economy has improved. State support for business and production has been cut, limited private enterprise reintroduced, centralized planning lessened, and foreign investment encouraged. As a result, family businesses have blossomed. Streets in Hanoi and Ho Chi Minh City are lined with small shops specializing in the sale of shoes, luggage, watches, and other consumer goods.

THE GENERAL SUCCESS OF *DOI MOI*

In 1991, when the Soviet Union collapsed, Vietnam barely avoided bankruptcy by further opening its markets to free trade. But improvement is slow and has not always been smooth. Vietnam remains a poor country. The end of communist state-run enterprises led to layoffs of workers, which raised the numbers of unemployed. Second-rate goods and equipment plague consumers who still turn to the black market to buy illegally imported goods.

Vietnam is no longer a completely closed society, however. Many restrictions have been lifted. For example, citizens and visitors may now travel freely within the country. Vietnamese who left the country for political or economic reasons are now encouraged, rather than forbidden, to re-

Vietnam slowly opened its markets to free trade after the collapse of the Soviet Union.

Vietnam now welcomes tourists and encourages foreign business.

turn to visit, make investments, or even live. As the outpouring of boat people nearly exhausted the resources and patience of Hong Kong and other countries like Malaysia that established refugee camps, Vietnam's new, open policy is welcome. About 110,000 Viet Kieu, as people who left Vietnam to live elsewhere are known in Vietnam, have been repatriated from refugee camps.

Tourists are likewise welcomed into Vietnam, as are overseas business enterprises. International businesses are encouraged to invest in partnership with Vietnamese companies, agencies, or local governments. Exploration for offshore oil and natural gas has piqued more than a little interest from foreign companies, and hotel and resort chains are springing up to accommodate new foreign interest in Vietnam.

The peasants are realizing some material gain, but still are not experiencing the prosperity accompanying various successful business ventures in the nation's urban centers. As a result, *doi moi* has also led to a migration of peasants seeking their fortunes in the cities, especially Ho Chi Minh City. Cities are crowded, noisy, and chaotic with the recent increase in cars, motorcycles, and people on bicycles or on foot. Streetside vendors may be seen alongside entrepreneurs with cellphones.

THE U.S. EMBARGO

After the Vietnam War, many members of the Association of Southeast Asian Nations (ASEAN) resumed their status as trade partners and recipients of significant aid from the United States. However, the United States, ASEAN nations, and many other Western nations refused to lift trade embargos imposed during the war against Vietnam.

Vietnam then turned to trade instead with its old communist ally, the USSR. The USSR stood ready to help as it had during the war, and yet was far enough away, unlike looming China, not to pose a threat. The USSR loaned billions in rubles to Vietnam, conferring on it a most favored nation status for carrying out communist-style industrialization, progress in agricultural production, and increasing public welfare, as part of Vietnam's second Five Year Plan (1976–1980). The Soviet Union used Vietnam's naval stations and airstrips for its own military buildup in the region.

In 1977, the Carter administration opened negotiations with Vietnam and dropped its opposition to Vietnam's membership in the United Nations. However, the negotiations failed under pressure from Vietnam for war reparations and from U.S. political groups demanding Vietnamese help in the search for missing American servicemen.

When Ronald Reagan, a fervent anticommunist, became president in 1980, the U.S. Treasury Department, under the Trading with the Enemy Act, prohibited American companies from engaging in any business enterprises with Vietnam. The Bush administration held to this stance.

With Vietnam's withdrawal from Cambodia and the fall of the USSR, U.S. allies such as Japan and France dropped their support for the embargo. In 1994, the Clinton administration finally lifted the embargo.

Some of this change is also reflected in village life. Lady Borton, a periodic resident of Vietnam, writes of the changes she observed in one village since *doi moi:*

> By early 1990, the peasants of Khanh Phu had reaped huge profits on their privately held rice paddies. The village had a zest I'd never felt before. . . . Like much of Viet Nam, Khanh Phu had entered the consumer age. Motorcycles, non existent in the village three years before, were common.[12]

While utilities and the media remain completely under state control, some public services such as health care and education are no longer provided by the state. Individuals must sometimes pay for health care, and parents must pay tuition for students above the third grade. Consequently, beggars still ask for money on city streets.

Economic growth rates, statistics that are used to show the increase in the monetary value of what a country has produced in a given year, show that Vietnam's economy is improving. Before *doi moi*, the growth rate was negative, but today Vietnam is one of fifteen countries claiming the highest growth rates in the world, and the nation enjoys trade relations with over one hundred countries.

LIFTING THE U.S. EMBARGO

In addition to the economic disasters brought about by its own internal policies, Vietnam was hampered after the Vietnam War by American trade embargos set in place during the conflict. The administrations of Presidents Ronald Reagan and George Bush prohibited trade between American companies and Vietnam. However, in February 1994 the United States lifted its trade embargo against Vietnam; five years later, President Bill Clinton signed an agreement to expand trade between Vietnam and America. Both nations stand to profit from increased trade.

Vietnam has traveled a bumpy economic road and still faces challenges in raising its standard of living. However, its government has proved adaptable and perceptive by its willingness to institute *doi moi*. Promising economic growth is the result.

5

DAILY LIFE:
ANCIENT RHYTHMS,
DIFFERENT DRUMMERS

Events of the past fifty years have brought many changes to Vietnamese society. The wars with France and the United States fragmented families and left numbers of children without one or both parents. More women are single now, due to shortages of partners since so many men died in the wars. A generation was left with the physical and mental scars of war. Even today, a serious and realistic fear, especially in rural areas, is that fieldworkers or children playing will be killed by stumbling on and accidentally detonating unexploded bombs. The bitterness of war memories is gradually fading, however, and Vietnamese youth are intrigued by Western, especially American, culture. They watch MTV and many like to wear jeans and T-shirts. Owning a motorbike is a status symbol in this traditionally nonmaterialistic and noncompetitive nation. Changes in the Vietnamese economy have led the young to question the advice and the practices of their elders more than Vietnamese youth would have done in the past. Some young adults live alone instead of with family, although these are still in a minority. Many young women are not as strictly chaperoned on social occasions as their mothers were. The young in Vietnam may go out dancing on occasion with no supervision at all.

PEASANT LIFE

Change is more obvious in Vietnam's cities than in the villages. Vietnam's peasant farmers, who make up 80 percent of the population, live today much as their ancestors lived centuries ago. Few families have indoor plumbing or cars and some villages also lack electricity. Boats, bicycles, and ox-drawn carts are the most common forms of transportation. Roads are often rough. In certain rural areas, bridges may be barely wide enough for an ox cart to cross. In southern Vietnam, for example, many village houses are reached over waterways by monkey bridges, so called because one needs the dexterity of a monkey to get across such a narrow little bridge.

As it has for centuries, the village marketplace holds a central role in rural life. Produce, animals, clothing, and other items are sold there and news of the day is exchanged. Also important is the dinh, a mix of temple and community center usually found in the middle of a village that serves as a spiritual and political gathering place

Vietnamese peasants typically begin their day at dawn, take a break during the heat of the day, then return to the fields until evening. Breakfast may consist of rice and fruit. Noon lunch may be cold rice and greens with green tea. Supper is often rice, vegetables, and perhaps a little meat with tea. After supper is the time for relaxing and socializing. The men may smoke pipes; the women chew betel nuts, a popular treat that has an effect similar to that of nicotine. Most

Peasant life in Vietnam today is not very different from peasant life centuries ago.

★ THE PEASANT HOME

Rural Vietnamese homes have common features. The main house is furnished simply with reed mat beds with mosquito netting where one or more family members sleep. Vietnamese do not like to be alone, so such close physical proximity is important. The house may contain a table or two and, always in the center, the family altar with photos or mementos for the household owner's ancestral worship. Incense is burned and prayers are offered there.

A peasant's home, once typically of bamboo and thatch construction now is often built of wood and stucco-covered bricks. Rainwater is collected for drinking in urns positioned beneath the house eaves; creek or river water is used for washing. A bathhouse may be separate from the house but near the river, with a wash slab, perhaps concrete, next to it. Most kitchens are also separate structures; food is cooked over a smoky wood or coal fire. A hammock might be stretched outside near the woodshed and pigsty.

Normally there will be an orchard of lush fruit such as jackfruit, plum, coconut, water apple, lemon, bananas, milk fruit, rambutan, or durium. The perfume of the trumpet-shaped white and gold frangipani blossom floats through the orchard and over a vegetable plot. Squash, okra, peppers, onions, soybeans, yams, and other foods grow there.

people retire early, and at night the sounds of rural Vietnam may be only cicadas, owls, and the rustling of bamboo or iron pine along nearby waters.

RICE

Work in the rural regions mostly revolves around rice and the cycles of rice production. As author Lady Borton says, "A peasant's years pass in a rhythm of seasons: transplant, weed, harvest, rest; transplant, weed, harvest, rest."[13] During the time of rest, ceremonial and social events such as weddings are scheduled.

The physically demanding and detailed nature of growing rice requires a collective effort. Communal cooperation and interdependence have long been a way of life for the peasants, perhaps one reason that many were initially willing to accept communism.

From planting seedlings in the paddies until harvest, growing rice is arduous. In addition to hard labor, raising a successful rice crop requires knowledge and skill. Mid-February begins one of three planting seasons. At this time farmers will have marked rows for planting by stakes driven into the mud below the water, and they will have plowed the paddy by guiding a water buffalo down the rows, slicing the harrow through water. Workers, usually women, bearing yoked shoulder baskets full of rice seedlings then step bare-foot into the waters of the paddy, each carrying a clump of seedlings. Each shoot is separated, and its fine roots planted in the mud below the water's surface. The workers move backward down each row, taking care to plant seedlings about a hand's length apart. Some wear leggings for protection from leeches.

The rice grows waist-high and looks like tall grass as the kernels mature. When the plants appear ready, about four months after transplanting, the paddies are drained of most of their water. A worker will gather two clumps of rice in one

Women irrigate a rice paddy near Hanoi. Rice is still the predominant crop in Vietnam's rural regions.

hand, twist a few stalks around the clump and cut the stems with a sickle. The clumps are then set aside, to be gathered into sheaves tied with bamboo strips.

In order to separate the grains from the plant, workers spread the plants over a flat, dry surface such as a courtyard, or even a paved road, and a heavy stone roller is pulled across the rice grains, to knock the grains loose from the stalks. Members of a group take turns pulling the stone in pairs.

Eventually, a worker will rake away the straw, leaving the rice kernels to dry in the sun. Finally, the good grain is swept up and is ready for consumption.

DRAMATIC CHANGES IN THE CITIES

Unlike rural life, life in Vietnam's cities has changed dramatically in the ten years since *doi moi* was introduced. Twenty percent of the population resides in the cities. Sports utility vehicles compete on crowded streets with cyclos, foot-drawn buggies, and motorbikes. City residents have seen their standard of living rise. Food is varied (even including pizza parlors) and plentiful in contrast to the hungry years of the 1980s. There are far fewer homeless. Since *doi moi*, both Hanoi and Ho Chi Minh City have experienced population growth and the proliferation of small businesses, many family owned. Foreigners visit as tourists or investors.

Despite the many successes of *doi moi*, unemployment remains high. Urban unemployment rates range from 6 to 11 percent. (It is believed that unemployment is even higher in rural areas.) The lingering Asian recession of the 1990s is

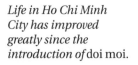

Life in Ho Chi Minh City has improved greatly since the introduction of doi moi.

largely responsible, causing a drop in overseas orders sent to Vietnamese factories that produce apparel and shoes. Even foreign-owned companies like Nike have been laying off workers. Economic difficulties in neighboring Asian countries have not helped the construction industry either. A construction boom that began in the 1980s has stalled as a result of the recession, and equipment sits idle by partially complete buildings. The government has pledged to offset unemployment by putting people to work on ambitious infrastructure and public works projects.

Natural disasters have played a part in interfering with both business and agriculture as well, including a drought in 1997–1998 and tropical storms such as Typhoon Linda.

Despite high unemployment, many urban Vietnamese still work long days, sometimes holding two jobs to pay for tiny, often shared apartments. Most have electricity, which means television sets are a common possession even in the smallest apartments, but cooking often takes place outside. Indoor plumbing is not universal, and personal grooming such as hair brushing often takes place outdoors. Children frequently shine shoes after school or do chores for the family business. Elderly people in both city and country look after small children.

Although decades have passed since the Vietnam War and the period of hard-line communism that followed, Vietnam still suffers from effects of both. A World Bank report indicates that about one-third of Vietnamese still live in poverty, although that figure is down from the 70 percent rate of 1980. Amputee beggars and begging children, as well as prostitutes, are a not uncommon sight, although government efforts have been made to curtail prostitution. Poverty, overpopulation, and recent natural disasters contribute to the current economic situation.

FAST-PACED URBAN CENTERS

A black market thrives in urban centers of Vietnam. One visitor to Hanoi remembers that the movie *Titanic* was available there on video via the black market before it was available in the United States. An illegal exotic animal trade also thrives and includes sale of such creatures as macaques and gibbons.

However, legitimate businesses thrive, too. In Hanoi's Old Quarter entire streets are devoted to specialized luxury goods: jewelry, watches, luggage, or silks. But it is unnecessary to own

In Hanoi's Old Quarter small businesses, including shopkeepers and peddlers, thrive.

a store in Vietnamese cities to peddle products. Many people sell their goods in stalls on the streets or even from shoulder yokes. Flower vendors, for example, sell their bouquets this way, biking into town at dawn loaded with flowers grown in village suburbs. Other merchants bake bread in the early morning and spend the day going from place to place to sell their loaves.

Ho Chi Minh City buzzes with the same activities as Hanoi, only more intensely with its population at 4 million and growing. A longtime trading center and the capital of South Vietnam when the American military and its money poured in, Ho Chi Minh City has taken up private enterprise again with gusto. There are no longer food shortages. Money flows in part because people who hoarded gold and dollars in 1975 are bringing them out again. Women are renewing their interest in fashion and makeup, and beauty salons are a common sight. Chinese in the suburb of Cholon, where trading is especially active, receive investments from Chinese friends and relatives throughout Southeast Asia.

Traffic in the narrow urban streets of Hanoi and Ho Chi Minh City is chaotic. Drivers pass on hills and curves, ignore red lights, and make U-turns, honking their horns constantly. The din of horns starts at about 6:00 A.M. and lasts until 11:00 at night. Vehicles include cyclos, which are pedicabs pulled by drivers on foot, bicycles, motorcycles, cars, and buses.

"I sat at my hotel window for about an hour, trying to figure out how to walk across the street," recalls Jim Soular, an American veteran who recently revisited Vietnam. "The worst mistake westerners make is to freeze part way across," he adds. "The drivers have seen you and gauged your speed. It throws everything off if you stop."[14]

Street life can also be a source of entertainment. Urban Vietnamese enjoy chess, cards, gambling, horse racing, and cockfighting. On Sundays, families will gather at favorite street intersections to watch or participate in some of these activities. Parents also take their children to city parks for play.

Traffic in the cities is a chaotic mixture of buses, cars, bicyclists, and pedicabs.

City parks featuring scenic lakes are where many urban Vietnamese gather to start the day. Following breakfast, typically a hot soup of noodles and spices with bits of beef or chicken, called pho, many city dwellers go to the park to practice tai chi, an ancient form of exercise. Some prefer to jog or play volleyball, badminton, soccer, or a sort of combination of the last two, shuttlecock, sometimes called Vietnam's national pastime. At about 7:00 A.M., loudspeakers installed by the communist government began to blare patriotic songs from nearly every downtown street corner. When outdoor morning exercise is concluded, parks are abandoned as the workday begins.

FAMILY STRUCTURE

Whether urban or rural, most people in Vietnam live in homes passed from one generation to the next, with extended families of three generations sharing one home. Houses and apartments tend to be small, sometimes only two rooms. Men and boys usually sleep in the front of the house near the ancestral altar, while women and girls sleep in the rear.

Children are considered a great blessing in Vietnamese culture. Although families used to have ten to fifteen children, in part as insurance that parents would be cared for in old age, few Vietnamese choose to have so large a family today. Government efforts to reduce population growth, as well as couples' desire to avoid the expense of raising and educating many children, have reduced birth rates. Urban families especially are apt to limit their children to two.

Children, especially girls, were and still are expected to contribute to the family by cooking, cleaning, and caring for younger brothers and sisters while their parents are at work. Boys are the preferred sex, however, as they can carry on the family name and, when their parents die, make offerings to their souls at the family ancestral altar. It is also the job of the oldest brother to guide and nurture his younger brothers and sisters, making sure, for example, that they do their chores and schoolwork. Younger siblings must obey and respect their older brothers. Although younger brothers are expected to contribute, it is the oldest brother on whom the great responsibility of caring for aged parents and paying homage to ancestors falls.

In the family hierarchy, men are heads of households and have primary responsibility for the family's support. However, women and men often work side by side to support the family. Vietnamese women contribute to the family through hard physical labor, or run businesses, or may be artisans in lacquerware or ceramics. But ideally, in Vietnamese society, they are also to be submissive to their husbands, and keep the households running smoothly by maintaining them as dutiful daughters, wives, and mothers should.

Women usually remain in their parental homes until marriage, which often happens in their early twenties. A young

STATUS OF WOMEN IN MODERN VIETNAM

Vietnamese men gather after work for tea, beer, and gossip at streetside stalls, but their wives have no similar respite. Although the Marriage and Family Act of 1959 declares that sons and daughters must be treated equally, and a 1986 act gives husbands and wives equal responsibility for child care and housework, these provisions are not followed in practice. Women work outside the home, then do household chores such as cooking (often done outside), laundry, cleaning, and seeing to children's needs. Men do, at times, play with their children or advise them on matters such as schoolwork.

Women also tend to be hired for seasonal work or lower-paying employment involving physical labor.

Women in Vietnam are primarily responsible for raising the children and maintaining the home.

woman's honor is important; she may have a curfew as early as 6:00 P.M., imposed by her parents until she marries. After marriage, a bride leaves to live with or near her husband's parents.

Grandparents help care for young children. Vietnamese grandparents and other elders are respected for their wisdom and the young seek their advice. However, as in any society where different generations live together, there is sometimes conflict. Being thrust into the modern world and exposed to more materialistic lifestyles has affected the generations to some extent. As author and former Vietnam resident Claire Ellis writes, "The fast changes in Vietnam's economy have seen this respect eroded a little and one of the few areas where younger members of the family contradict their elders is with regard to today's market forces."[15]

RELIGION

Nearly every Vietnamese home, even if it is a crowded urban apartment, has a centrally placed altar. This ancestral

THE BETROTHAL CEREMONY AND WEDDING

If all bodes well, the first step toward marriage is the betrothal ceremony. A procession leaves from the future groom's house bearing gifts for the bride in special red-wrapped boxes. The gifts include jewelry, areca nuts, and betel leaves, which represent conjugal love. The bride's family also receives gifts: altar candles, fruit, whiskey. If groom and gifts are acceptable, a fortune teller will set the time for the wedding, traditionally three years into the future.

On the day of the wedding, a master of ceremonies leads a delegation from the groom's house to the bride's house, where firecrackers explode prior to their entry. The groom and his party then go to the bride and present her with flowers, adorn her with jewelry, and give her two large candles. The couple and their families and guests drink whiskey and feast. The wedding and reception, held at the groom's father's house, are hours long. Speeches are given and photographs taken. The bride changes her dress many times and each new outfit calls for another photograph. There may be dancing. It is considered bad luck for the couple to spend their wedding night anywhere but in the groom's father's house.

Vietnamese family life is important and still rather traditional.

altar serves as a shrine where incense and offerings, such as money, or paper replicas of desirable items, such as cars, are burned as gifts to be sent on to the ancestor. The altar is usually adorned with photographs of the ancestors or, if none are available, small objects that an ancestor owned.

Ancestor worship is the oldest spiritual practice in Vietnam, part of the life of most people regardless of whether they identify themselves as adherents of any other religious

belief. Vietnamese revere their ancestors, who, they believe, continue to bless and protect their descendants.

Love and attention are vital to the well-being of ancestors. If the deceased are neglected, they are eternally restless. Ghosts, those uneasy souls of the dead whose graves are untended, wander the land and may appear as human beings. Ghosts are accorded great respect as they are thought to be capable of stealing a person's heart and soul.

Ancestor worship is only one of the spiritual practices found in Vietnam today. Although the communist government at first officially discouraged organized religion, many Vietnamese retained their traditional beliefs. About two-thirds of those who practice religion today are Buddhists. Many do not adhere to Buddhism alone, however. Religion in Vietnam often blends various religious and spiritual teachings. This mix is described by historian Stanley Karnow:

Buddhism remains the primary religion of Vietnam.

[The Vietnamese] venerate scholars rather than priests, seeking harmony in the present rather than salvation in a hereafter. Thus they put a premium on ethics rather than on faith, and they can blend elements of Buddhism, Confucianism, and Taoism, their three pillars of wisdom, with animism, superstition, various forms of magic, idolatry, and above all, ancestor worship.[16]

Animism, the ancient and widespread belief that spirits inhabit natural or man-made objects such as clouds, trees, kitchens, or rivers, is seen in many superstitions and ceremonies. For example, at the start of Tet, the Vietnamese New Year, each household holds a ceremony in honor of the household gods, who will go to heaven to report on each household member's behavior during the past year. Between the departure of the protective household gods and the arrival of their replacements, much noise is made, usually with fireworks, to frighten away evil spirits.

Christianity, too, is practiced in Vietnam. About 10 percent of the Vietnamese population are Christian, most of those Roman Catholic.

LIFE'S MILESTONES

Besides the rituals of worship in the pagoda, church, or Vietnamese home's ancestral altar, other traditions marking life's milestones are widely followed. Although wedding ceremonies may vary depending on regional differences, some rituals hold nearly everywhere. Parental approval matters and a couple may be forbidden to wed due to class differences or inauspicious astrologic signs.

Another fundamental ritual of human life—the funeral—adheres to ancient customs. It is appropriate for a person to die at home, not in a hospital. Processions of mourners in white accompany the dead to the gravesite. A period of mourning in which the relatives do not visit pagodas, attend festivals, dress in bright colors, or marry, follows. The length of mourning varies with circumstances. Three years after the burial, the deceased is exhumed in a ceremony known as the Washing of the Shirt. Because of the watery ground of Vietnam, all that remains by that time is a skeleton. The bones and skull are scrubbed clean by male relatives and put in a small earthenware container to be placed on ancestral land.

Such traditions bespeak an ancient culture that respects the past. Vietnamese people have a history of valuing close

CARING FOR ANCESTORS

A neglected grave is a serious disgrace and causes anguish for the dead. Not surprisingly, it is extremely important that one's descendants care for one's grave. During the Lunar New Year festival, or Tet, the family cleans weeds away from ancestral graves.

A male family member is assigned to care for both the ancestral gravesite and a plot of land that provides income for ancestral offerings, which take various forms. For example, on a street in Hanoi's Old Quarter called Paper Street, people buy paper replicas of anything they think might be of comfort to the dead: money, paper houses, motorcycles, cars. These are burned to send them on their way to the ancestors.

Incense is burned at the central ancestral altar in nearly any Vietnamese home on certain occasions, especially the anniversary of the ancestor's death. Pagodas frequently have rows of photographs and memorial tablets for honoring the deceased.

CAODAISM

Cao Dai, founded in the 1920s by a civil servant named Ngo Minh Chiu, emerged as a sect that melds the teachings of Buddhism, Confucianism, Taoism, Christianity, and the best of secular teachings. Its saints are a quixotic mix that includes Joan of Arc, Shakespeare, Christ, Buddha, Victor Hugo, Winston Churchill, and Charlie Chaplin. Pageantry, seances, and a colorful temple appeal to the masses. The Cao Dai had its own territory and a private army until it met resistance from the Diem regime. It has made a comeback in the South, however, and now has an estimated 2 million followers.

Worshipers attend a Cao Dai mass.

family ties and spiritual harmony. But the nation is facing rapid change as a result of both exposure to the West and a changing economy. While the change is positive in terms of economic well-being, it is such economic change that brings about emphasis on individual, competitive private enterprise and the pursuit of modern material possessions, sometimes to the point of sacrificing old ways of life. In deciding how to live today, thoughtful Vietnamese seek a balance between the old culture and new opportunities for prosperity.

6

Arts and Culture

Art and culture in Vietnam are rich in beauty and symbolism. The love of beauty pervades people's lives in various ways, as it has done for thousands of years. Vietnamese celebrate beauty and symbolism most happily in their popular festivals. Villages, temples, and pagodas observe annual festivals, frequently in spring, and visitors come to enjoy processions, rituals, special foods, and entertainment. Festivals are often held to honor deities and national heroes, and to celebrate love.

THE LUNAR TET

The most important festival in Vietnam marks the Lunar New Year, Tet Ca, called Tet. *Tet* is a Chinese word which means a new meteorological period of the year. It is believed that the passing from one period to another can cause natural disturbances like heat, rain, or mist that must be exorcised in ritual and festivals. Though many Tets are celebrated each year, the primary Tet takes place at some time in the end of January or the first part of February, about halfway between winter solstice and spring equinox. It is a celebration of communion, renewal, and peace.

After twelve months, both the peasant and the rice paddy need and enjoy a rest and so, in part, Tet is about seasonal communion with nature. Tet also represents the communion of family members and villages. At this time of year, people try to return home to be with extended family and close friends, eat special foods, and exchange good wishes and small gifts. Tet also means the communion of all citizens. While president, Ho Chi Minh wrote Tet greetings to the nation, which he read over the radio at midnight on each Tet Eve. His poems reflected the challenges and progress of the country.

Tet is celebrated for three days. On the eve of Tet, prayers are offered at ancestral altars and visits made to temples and pagodas. Exploding fireworks cause a deafening racket. On the first day, the first sound heard is significant. A dog barking is a good omen, while a rooster's crow foretells a hard year. The first visitor to the house also foreshadows good or bad luck. Arrangements are often made in advance for a gifted or especially fortunate person, such as one with many children, to visit first. Visiting and feasting continue throughout Tet.

As the festival arrives just before spring, Tet also celebrates renewal and rebirth. During Tet, a person's actions should stem from good will, as this will predict his or her actions for the coming year. After the holiday, Vietnamese resume daily life refreshed and optimistic, and the renewing spirit of Tet lingers throughout lesser festivals that continue through spring.

Here, residents in Hanoi gather for Tet, a three-day festival to celebrate the New Year.

THE VIETNAMESE LOVE OF BEAUTY

The Vietnamese appreciation for beauty is not limited to the celebration and symbolism of festivals. The arts are keenly valued as well. Vietnam's skilled painters, musicians, writers, and craftspeople command international respect and Vietnam has contributed through import and export to the arts of all Asia, and now to the West as well. Artifacts such as ceramics, tapestries, even fashion, find their way to collectors in Europe and America. In turn, the styles and techniques of other countries have influenced the arts in Vietnam.

Because of Vietnam's climate, which can be ruinous to materials less durable than stone or bronze, most of the oldest art that has survived is in the form of sculpture or stelae, which are inscribed stone pillars or upright slabs. The most ancient artifacts that have survived the triple threat of heat, humidity, and war are the Bronze Age Dongsonian rain drums, so called because they are believed to have been used to encourage and celebrate the arrival of rain while imitating the sound of thunder. They are admired for their intricate relief carvings.

HANDICRAFTS

Ceramics has ancient roots in Vietnam as well. Chinese influences dating back centuries are visible in Vietnamese pottery in terms of both form and style. An example is the delicate blue and white porcelain produced in both countries in the fifteenth and sixteenth centuries. But Vietnamese work is still recognizably Vietnamese in its designs, quality, and energetic brushstrokes. A spirit of humor and fun often blends with skilled artistry.

Vietnamese potters have long experimented with distinctive glazes, patterns, and finishes. During the eleventh and twelfth centuries, for example, Vietnamese potters specialized in brown glaze on white; in the thirteenth and fourteenth centuries they favored monochromatic glazes of green, white, or brown. In the fifteenth century, Muslim traders introduced the ingredient cobalt. Blue and white designs from the soft Hue blue to the brighter shades from Bat Trang gained and held popularity.

Pottery made in the Red River Delta at kiln centers such as Bat Trang have gained international notice for the blending of ancient techniques of firing and design with innovative patterns and finishes. Entire families, about two thousand in Bat Trang alone, work together to fuel kilns for firing the ceramics and to complete the designs. Although the best of these artisans are not widely known by name, some families do boast of having master craftspeople in their midst.

Vietnamese artisans are known for the production of another ancient art form called lacquerware, also of Chinese origin but now found throughout Vietnam. Lacquer work originated in ancient times as a technique to waterproof barges, but in the fifteenth century artisans adapted the process for decorative purposes. A wood (often teak) box, vase, or other object is covered in ten layers of resin from the cay son tree. Each layer dries for a week, then the artist sands it. After an eleventh coat is applied, it is sanded with a special coal powder and lime wash, then decorated. The lacquer can have a black tint or the golden brown called cockroach wing. Designs are engraved, painted, or created by insets of mother of pearl, eggshell,

Vietnamese ceramics, like this funerary urn (left) and decorated clay plate, are recognizable by their design, quality, and brushstroke.

gold, or silver. Lacquerware is a popular item with tourists, who especially like to purchase sets of nesting boxes. As is the case with ceramics, artisans are not apt to achieve individual fame for their work.

Artisans work with wood not only in lacquerware, but also in the folk art of woodblock prints. Created by the peasants of Ho village in Bac Ninh Province, the art of woodblock printing has been revived since national unification. Brightly colored drawings are engraved on wood, then printed on hand-made paper coated with white oyster shell powder. Drawings such as one entitled "The Sow and the Piglets" denote prosperity, while other subjects celebrate national heroes like the Trung sisters or praise morality, or satirize human folly. In short, the pictures are bright, cheerful depictions of the common Vietnamese peasant or laborers' outlook. These optimistic drawings are especially popular during the national holiday of Lunar Tet.

VISUAL ARTS FROM SILK TO CANVAS

Fabric arts are also part of Vietnam's artistic heritage. Tapestries with finely stitched detail display scenes of heroes or nature. Another art form involving fabric, silk painting, began in the thirteenth century. Scholar-artists brushed calligraphy and landscapes on frame-mounted silk. Some modern painters have returned to silk painting. Some, like Dau Mai, especially known for nudes, paint with watercolor on silk; others like Duong Tuan Duc, whose work is in private collections throughout the world, paint landscapes and other subjects with oil on silk.

Art schools have been established in Hanoi, Hue, and Ho Chi Minh City, and the styles and subjects of their graduates' work varies widely. One artist, Le Thanh Minh, paints on bark paper, depicting nudes in beautiful natural settings, often with images of Buddha. His themes raise questions about the proper conduct of life, of how to deal with good and evil.

Many of Vietnam's well-known painters depict themes of resistance struggles. For example, the face of Ho Chi Minh nearly always appears somewhere on the canvasses of contemporary painter Nguyen Quan.

PERFORMING
WITH WATER PUPPETS

Originally village entertainment, water puppetry was performed for royalty beginning in the twelfth century. Today the tradition is revived by state-supported troupes whose performances are a favorite with tourists. Dressed in costumes over wetsuits, puppeteers stand behind a curtain in water up to their thighs and manipulate several doll-size puppets by means of submerged bamboo poles. Firecrackers, churning water, and smoke accompany battles, folktales, and humorous scenes from village life. Musicians sing and play bamboo flutes, xylophones, drums, and gongs.

Being a puppeteer requires skill, strength, and commitment. An apprentice spends a six-year training period in stage work, movement, acting, and singing before becoming a troupe puppeteer.

Water puppetry is a uniquely Vietnamese tradition.

WATER PUPPETS

The Vietnamese value performance arts as much as they value the visual arts. Puppetry has long been one of the country's most popular performance arts. A distinct type, water puppetry, is performed in open air with a pond of water for the stage. The audience sits at the edge of the pond. An exploding firecracker usually announces the show's beginning and the puppets are manipulated from a room that is partially submerged in water. The puppeteers make the colorful puppets move across the surface by an underwater system of rods and strings. Frames with pulleys may connect many strings for complicated parade scenes. Water puppets are made of light, laquered wood, and communicate the story by gestures. The characters are often national heroes, but may also be ordinary workers, spirits, or animal figures.

Water puppetry actually originated in Vietnam in the Red River Delta region. One theory is that during flooding, innovative puppeteers with the attitude that the show must go on simply stepped into water up to their waists and water puppetry was born. "The water puppets," Susan Brownmiller writes, "are pure buffoon vaudeville that is unselfconsciously philosophic about the powerful forces of nature and war, a perfectly harmonious art form for a uniquely riparian [water-connected] warrior nation."[17]

POETRY AND PROSE

The themes of nature and war also appear in Vietnamese literature along with themes of love, friendship, family, and politics. Literature, whether poetry or prose, is traditionally of immense importance in Vietnamese culture. People often express themselves with poetry, either original or memorized.

During the Lunar Tet festival, for example, people buy a two-line verse expressing hopes or advice to place on family altars. A typical verse, for example, is, "On the Eve of New Year, debts are paid on every side; bending one's leg, one kicks out poverty."[18]

Folk poems, also popular in Vietnam, are written in couplets, two-line verses characterized by rhyme, metric rhythm, and tonal regularity. Tonal qualities are inflections of the voice, such as rising, falling, hardness, or softness, that add complexity to the spoken word. The Vietnamese language, though largely monosyllabic, is six-toned, and so a word can have entirely different meanings depending on the tone with which it is spoken. Thus, tone is as important in poetry as rhyme and meter. Regularity of these three elements have made long stretches of verse easy to memorize and recite.

VIETNAMESE NAMES

Vietnamese names are often poetic. The family or clan name comes first. Traditional middle names indicate gender (Van for men, Thi for women). An individual's given name has special meaning. Boys are given names that denote a desirable quality like Vigor, Virtue, or Modesty. Girls are given a name that signifies beauty such as Phoenix, or Perfume, or Blossom. Children may be named after birth order as well. Symbolism also appears in nicknames, often intentionally ugly or undesirable like Bear or Cow, to keep evil spirits from taking an interest and snatching lovely children away.

Reverence for literature has translated to high regard for writers and poets. Writers and poets have not always been able to freely express themselves, however. One contemporary novelist, Duong Thu Huong, saw her work both admired and censored because she expressed opinions on political and social concerns. She began writing during the Vietnam War, organizing musical shows for northern troops and composing songs and poems. After the war, she became a screenwriter for the Hanoi Feature Film Studio, where her first work, a satire, was banned by the government. However, in 1979, after the Chinese invasion of Vietnam, she wrote a strongly anti-Chinese screenplay that won her acclaim.

But in 1980, Huong began to write short stories and also to object publicly to government censorship of her work. Although she joined the Communist Party in 1984, six years later she was expelled for her blunt criticisms of the regime. Her novel *Paradise of the Blind*, which concerned the brutal purges in North Vietnam under communism in the 1950s, was published, then later withdrawn from circulation by the government. In 1991, in connection with a conspiracy against the communist government, she was imprisoned for seven months. Huong is free now, and photocopies of her book circulate in secret. Internationally respected, this author continues to speak out against whatever she sees as injustice.

Another popular writer is Bao Ninh. In 1991, he won Vietnam's highest literary award, the Writers' Union Award for Best Fiction, for *The Sorrows of War*. The novel is about the hardships and horrors of war and its aftermath as experienced by a young North Vietnamese soldier.

The most beloved masterpiece of Vietnamese literature is a long narrative poem, *The Tale of Kieu,* by Nhuyen Du (1765–1820). In the epic poem, beautiful Kieu, who is in love with a poet, sells herself to save the family honor and free her father from debtor's prison. She does not realize it will mean a life of prostitution for her. After many misadventures, she is restored to her family.

The story is known by heart by peasants and scholarly Vietnamese alike; a copy exists in most schools and homes throughout the country. It is cherished because it is a love story that also involves family loyalty, courage, and self-sacrifice.

MUSIC AND DANCE

As much as Vietnamese delight in their literary heritage and contemporary writings, they also love music. Contributions from various cultures have enriched the country's musical traditions. Traditional opera, for example, shows influences from China. Folk songs and dance reflect the mix of other peoples who have settled in different regions of Vietnam.

The five-note scale of Chinese origin prevails in the North, while a nine-note scale brought in by the Khmer (Cambodians) and Cham prevails in the South. The six-tone element of the language affects musical compositions in that the melody and word tones must correspond. A tonal language is one in which, unlike English, the speaker's inflection ac-

LEGEND OF THE HOUSEHOLD GODS

A famous Vietnamese legend tells of the three household gods. A childless wife left her dissatisfied husband and remarried. Her remorseful first husband searched for her until he was nearly blind and reduced to begging. When he came to her new home, she fed him, then hid him under a heap of straw as he slept. When her second husband lit the straw, he accidentally burned the first husband to death. She threw herself into the flames, followed by her grief-stricken second husband. Sorry for all three, the Emperor of Jade decreed from his heavenly kingdom that they would be household gods. Now the name Ong (Master) is given to the two rear stones and Ba (Madam) to the front stone of the traditional cooking-fire trestle.

tually changes the meaning of the word. Thus, in music, if a word has a rising tone, the melody cannot fall.

A popular singer of the traditional form known as ca tru, in which a poem is sung, is Kim Dzung. Her lyrics reflect happy themes concerning family, peace, and Vietnam.

A revival of interest in traditional music has seen its performances in cabarets, as dinner music in restaurants, and performances in hotels. Classic stringed instruments, drums, and flutes may be played alone or as accompaniment to dance or opera.

Each of Vietnam's minority populations has its own distinctive dance. For example, the M'nong people specialize in gong dances, while the Thai people move in a swaying motion enhanced by dancing on a springy bamboo floor. The Muong show their style by clapping bamboo sticks together to accompany their Sap Dance.

Music is a cherished art form to the Vietnamese.

Other, less traditional forms of music and dance have also caught on in Vietnam. The Vietnamese are becoming internationally recognized for accomplishments in classical ballet. Ballroom dancing and disco have become popular after being banned from 1975 until 1986. And rock music has also attracted a following in Vietnam. Singer-guitarist Pham Duy wrote and performed songs in the late 1960s and 1970s about the hardships of war. Rock music became popular during that time and groups such as CBC, the Strawberry Four, and the Blackstones were hits. Rock and roll remains popular in Vietnam today.

FASHION AND THE AO DAI

Fashion, cooking, and flower growing also provide pleasure to beauty-conscious Vietnamese. The traditional costume of choice for women, the ao dai, combines comfort for the wearer with charm for the viewer. It is a two-piece outfit. The top is a high-necked, long-sleeved tunic, usually knee length and slit on the sides to just below the bustline. Wide-legged trousers that touch the ground complete the ao dai. School-girls wear white ao dai, young working women wear pastels, and married women wear bright or dark-colored tunics over white or black trousers.

Dress indicates economic or ethnic distinctions. Urban women who do physical labor and peasants wear a loose top and baggy trousers called an ao ba ba. The ethnic minorities of the Central Highlands are known for their colorful woven fabric and sarongs.

The Chinese introduced the first version of the ao dai. Its present form appeared in 1930. The influence of the ao dai can now by seen in the work of fashion designers in the United States and Europe.

Here, a mother and daughter wear ao dai, the traditional costume for women.

THE ART OF GOOD FOOD

One of the lasting benefits of Vietnam's history of foreign occupation is its culinary legacy. Food, especially seafood,
fresh fruit, and vegetables, is now abundant in Vietnam and
Vietnamese chefs have adapted the best of culinary arts
from foreign sources. The country's cuisine has embraced
techniques such as stir-fry cooking from the Chinese and
hot pot cooking from Mongolia. The French introduced
crusty bread, caramelized sauces, banana flambé, and white
potatoes.

Buddhist vegetarian influences have led to especially fine
preparations of greens. Lettuce, onions, chickpeas, and bamboo shoots are just a few of the greens and legumes available
in Vietnam. Lemongrass, coconut milk, and nuoc mam, a
fermented anchovy sauce, are also common ingredients.
Vietnamese cookies may be made of bananas, egg, or coconut. Rice is served in different combinations with fruit,
vegetables, and beef or chicken. Rice is even fermented to
produce rice wine.

*Good food is now
plentiful in Vietnam.
Here, a couple enjoys a
traditional meal in a
city restaurant.*

FLOWERS, FLOWERS EVERYWHERE

Flower growing and arranging is a strong element of the Vietnamese love of beauty. Flowers grow in bright, lush splendor, perfuming the air of this hot, humid country. Frangipani flourishes, as do lilies, camellias, narcissus, chrysanthemums, peonies, roses, orchids, lotus, and hibiscus, to name just a few. They are brought to dinner parties by guests, and placed on ancestral altars.

Flowers can be symbolic. For example, a white narcissus symbolizes success and prosperity. Chrysanthemums are considered noble because they can survive cold weather. Peach blossoms symbolize faithfulness because of three historic warriors who swore fidelity to one another in a peach tree garden and kept their oath.

Vietnamese people's love of beauty is ancient and firmly ingrained. It comes from many sources, but the various art forms have evolved into styles that are distinctly Vietnamese in character—many steeped and refined in valued tradition, others the product of modern artists exploring various techniques and subjects. In art, in religion, in every aspect of their lives, the Vietnamese are a blend of tradition and transition, distinct and enduring.

FACTS ABOUT VIETNAM

GOVERNMENT:

Official name: Socialist Republic of Vietnam

National anthem: "Tien Quan Ca" ("Marching to the Front")

Flag: Single gold star centered on a red ground; the color red memorializes those who sacrificed their lives in the fight for independence and the star leads the people forward to the future.

Government: Vietnam is a socialist state under the leadership of the Vietnam Communist Party. The party holds chapter meetings at the local level. A national congress of delegates elects the Party Central Committee, which elects the powerful Politburo. The Central Committee has approximately 125 members and 50 alternates, and the Politburo is usually comprised of about 12 full members with perhaps 3 alternates. These numbers may vary from one Party Congress to the next. The party secretary-general chairs the Politburo, which watches over policy, directs the work of the ministries, and initiates laws for the National Assembly to consider.

National Assembly members serve for five-year terms. Candidates are proposed by the Communist Party, or by various social organizations known collectively as the Fatherland Front, or they may propose themselves, acting as independents. The Assembly has 450 members and meets three times a year. Ninety percent of the current Assembly are communists. In addition to its main purpose of passing laws, the Assembly appoints a prime minister and cabinet, and elects the president.

Each government department is headed by one of nineteen ministers.

There are sixty-one provinces, plus one special zone (Vung Tau) and three special municipalities: Ho Chi Minh City, Hanoi, and Haiphong. Each province is divided into municipalities, towns, districts, and villages. Local government is administered by people's councils, who appoint people's committees.

Independence: September 2, 1945

Reunification: July 2, 197695

Voting age: 18

Judicial: The judicial system comprises the Supreme People's Court, provincial courts, and district courts. The president of the Supreme Court is responsible to the National Assembly, as is the procurator-general, who heads the Supreme People's Office of Supervision and Control.

NATIONAL HOLIDAYS

January 1	New Year's Day
February 3	Establishment of the Vietnamese Communist Party in 1930
April 30	Liberation of South Vietnam
May 1	International Labor Day
May 19	Ho Chi Minh's Birthday
September 2	Vietnam National Day, also known as Independence Day
December 25	Christmas Day

GEOGRAPHY

Area: 329,560 km^2 (about 127,242 mi^2)

Cities: Capital, Hanoi (3.5 million); Ho Chi Minh City, formerly Saigon (5 million); Haiphong (1.5 million)

Terrain: Mountainous to coastal delta

Climate: All of Vietnam is in the tropical zone, but weather patterns vary. A humid monsoon climate provides tropical conditions in the South with a rainy season from May to October. The subtropical conditions in the North can turn wintry when polar air moves south over Asia.

Hanoi: Coldest month is January with an average temperature of 16.5 ºC (61.7ºF); hottest months are June to August with an average June temperature of 28.8 ºC (83.8ºF).

Ho Chi Minh City: Coldest month is January with an average mean temperature of 25.8 ºC (78.4ºF); hottest month is April with an average of 28.9 ºC (84.0ºF).

Annual rainfall: 72 inches

Rivers: Key rivers are the Red River in the North and the Mekong River in the South. These create the fertile deltas which make Vietnam the third-largest rice producer in the world.

Natural resources: Phosphates, coal, manganese, bauxite, chromate, offshore oil deposits, forests, rubber, marine products.

Agriculture and forestry (25 percent of gross domestic product, 1997) products: Rice, rubber, fruit, vegetables, corn manioc, cashews, sugar cane, coffee, fish.

Cultivated land: Less than 7 million hectares per year. Land use is 21 percent arable, 28 percent forest and woodland, 51 percent other.

PEOPLE:

Ethnic groups: Vietnamese (85–90 percent), Chinese, Hmong, Thai, Khmer, Cham, mountain groups.

Population: 77 million

Annual growth rate: 1.9 percent

Religions: Buddhism (with influence of Confucianism and Taoism),

Hao Hao, Cao Dai, Christian (mainly Roman Catholic, but with a Protestant minority), Animism, Islam. Ancestor worship is still widespread.

Literacy: 93 percent

Health: Birth rate, 28/1000; Infant mortality rate, 36/1000. Life expectancy: 63 years for men; 67 years for women. Medical facilities in 1991 included 1,550 hospitals, 10,710 medical centers, and 115 sanatoria.

INTERNATIONAL RELATIONS

Vietnam is a member the United Nations and the Association of South East Asian Nations.

ECONOMY

Gross domestic product (GDP): $25.6 billion

Per capita income: $320

Inflation rate: 3.6 percent

Under renovation, or *doi moi*, free enterprise principles have been partially implemented and central control reduced.

Unit of currency: dong

Banking and finance: The central bank and bank of issue is the National Bank of Vietnam. Vietnam has 52 commercial banks, 19 foreign branches, and 4 joint ventures set up with foreign capital. Vietcombank is the foreign trade bank. Fifty foreign banks have branches in Vietnam.

Trade unions: 53

NOTES

CHAPTER 1: THE GEOGRAPHY AND CLIMATE OF VIETNAM

1. Susan Brownmiller, *Seeing Vietnam: Encounters of the Road and Heart.* New York: HarperCollins, 1994, p. 16.

2. Quoted in Michael S. Yamashita, *Mekong: A Journey on the Mother of Waters.* New York: Takarajima, 1995, p. 11.

3. Yamashita, *Mekong,* p. 113.

4. Quoted in Yamashita, *Mekong,* p. 114.

CHAPTER 2: A LAND OF MANY INFLUENCES

5. Quoted in Stanley Karnow, *Vietnam: A History.* New York: Viking, 1983, p. 107.

6. Karnow, *Vietnam,* p. 99.

7. Quoted in Karnow, *Vietnam,* p. 103.

CHAPTER 3: FOREIGN DOMINATION AND INDEPENDENCE

8. Quoted in Karnow, *Vietnam,* p. 76.

9. Quoted in Lady Borton, *After Sorrow: An American Among the Vietnamese.* New York: Kodansha America, 1996, p. 62.

10. Quoted in Karnow, *Vietnam,* p. 135.

11. Quoted in Karnow, *Vietnam,* p. 374.

CHAPTER 4: AN ECONOMY IN TRANSITION

12. Borton, *After Sorrow,* p. 225.

CHAPTER 5: DAILY LIFE: ANCIENT RHYTHMS, DIFFERENT DRUMMERS

13. Borton, *After Sorrow,* p. 213.

14. Jim Soular, personal interview, Kalispell, Montana, June 20, 1999.

15. Claire Ellis, *Culture Shock! Vietnam: A Guide to Customs and Etiquette*. Portland: Graphic Arts Center, 1995, p. 59.

16. Karnow, *Vietnam*, p. 278.

CHAPTER 6: ARTS AND CULTURE

17. Brownmiller, *Seeing Vietnam*, p. 65.

18. Dick Van, "The Parallel Sentences," in *Vietnam, Cultural Window*. Hanoi: Giay, October 24, 1997, p. 18.

CHRONOLOGY

B.C.

2000
Northern Vietnam is the center of the Dong Son Bronze Age civilization.

700
A succession of eighteen Hung kings rule over the Lac Viet.

208
Chinese General Trieu Da betrays China, conquers Au Lac in the northern mountains, sets up a capital, and declares himself emperor of Nam Viet.

First century
Nam Viet becomes the province of Giao Chi, part of the Chinese empire during the Han dynasty.

A.D.

40
Trung sisters defeat the Chinese and found an independent state.

43
Chinese defeat the Trung sisters and their followers and reassert Chinese domination.

544
Ly Nam De leads his rebellion against China.

938
Ngo Quyen drives out the Chinese and establishes the first Vietnamese dynasty.

1009–1225
The Ly dynasty rules.

1010
Thang Lang, "Soaring Dragon," later to be called Hanoi, becomes the first capital of Vietnam.

1225–1288
Vietnamese successfully repel three Mongol invasions.

1407–1427
China, during the Ming dynasty, occupies Vietnam.

1428
Emperor Le Loi signs an accord with China that recognizes Vietnam's independence.

1460–1498
Le Thang Tong rules, revises the legal system, and expands his rule southward.

1545
Nearly two centuries of civil strife and internal power struggles begin.

1627
French Jesuit missionary Alexandre de Rhodes writes a grammar of Vietnamese using Roman alphabet, called quoc ngu. This marks the beginning of French influence in Vietnam.

1787
French missionary Pigniau de Behane asks Louis XVI to send miltary aid to help Nguyen Anh to gain the throne. France agrees to do so in exchange for exclusive trade privileges, then reneges on its agreement. French mercenaries chartered by Behane ally themselves with Nguyen Anh.

1802
Nguyen Anh (Gia Long) becomes emperor and unifies Vietnam.

1858
French troops attack Danang. French aggression will continue for decades.

1884
France regards Vietnam as a three-part country and treats the middle and northern sections—Annam and Tonkin— as a protectorate and Cochinchina in the south as a colony. In fact, harsh French rule is imposed over all Vietnam.

1890

Ho Chi Minh, revolutionary leader and the father of modern Vietnam, is born.

1930

Ho Chi Minh and others found the Vietnamese Communist Party; uprisings against the French increase.

1940

Occupation by Germany's ally, Japan, after Germany invades France; Ho Chi Minh forms the Vietminh to fight Japan and the French.

1945

Between 1 and 2 million Vietnamese starve; on September 2, Ho Chi Minh declares Vietnam's independence.

1946

Vietnam's war with France begins.

1954

The French are defeated at Dien Bien Phu. Vietnam is divided; national elections are scheduled for 1956.

1955

The United States sends military advisers to Vietnam.

1954–1960

Diem refuses to hold elections; land reforms in the North include tribunals carrying out a purge and many executions.

1960

The Ho Chi Minh Trail is used to bring aid to Viet Cong; Ho Chi Minh forms the National Liberation Front.

1963

The first Buddhist monk sets himself on fire to protest the Diem regime's tactics; Ngo Dinh Diem is assassinated.

1964

The U.S. embargo against North Vietnam begins; Congress passes the Tonkin Gulf Resolution; America bombs North Vietnam.

1968

North Vietnamese and Viet Cong carry out the siege of Khe Sanh and the Tet Offensive. Paris peace talks begin.

1969
President Richard Nixon begins "Vietnamization" of the
war; Ho Chi Minh dies.

1972
Nixon orders the "Christmas Bombing" of the North; Communists agree to resume peace talks.

1973
The Paris Peace Agreement is signed; American troops
withdraw; both sides return prisoners.

1975
North Vietnamese troops move south and capture Saigon;
Vietnam is reunified; the United States imposes a trade
embargo against Vietnam.

1977
The United Nations admits Vietnam as its 149th member.

1978
Vietnam joins Comecon, the East European economic
community; Cambodian Khmer Rouge move into southern
Vietnam; Vietnamese troops enter Cambodia.

1979
China, Cambodia's ally, invades Vietnam, but is rebuffed by
Vietnamese troops; Vietnam adopts a new constitution;
boat people's departures reach a new height.

1986
Renovation (*doi moi*) begins, combining a partial free market economy, greater everyday freedoms, and a more open
attitude toward the rest of the world.

1988
American and Vietnamese work together to locate the remains of missing U.S. soldiers.

1990
The last Vietnamese troops withdraw from Cambodia.

1994
The United States lifts trade embargo against Vietnam.

1995
Formal diplomatic relations between Vietnam and the United
States are reestablished with the exchange of ambassadors.

Suggestions For Further Reading

Hal Dureff, *The Story of Vietnam.* New York: Parents Magazine Press, 1966. Basic information about Vietnam for children.

Claire Ellis, *Culture Shock! Vietnam: A Guide to Customs and Etiquette.* Portland: Graphic Arts Center, 1995. Ellis has an insider's knowledge of modern Vietnam, including its history and culture.

Rick Graetz, assisted by Fred Rohrbach, *Vietnam: Opening Doors to the World.* Helena, MT: American Geographic Publishing, 1988. Although he visited Vietnam before *doi moi*, Graetz provides good information regarding geography and people in postwar Vietnam along with excellent maps and photographs.

Bill McCloud, *What Should We Tell Our Children About Vietnam?* Norman: University of Oklahoma Press, 1989. American citizens, including former presidents, officials, war protestors, and veterans, attempt to answer that question as it pertains to the war in Vietnam.

Nhuong Huynh Quang, *The Land I Lost.* New York: Harper and Row, 1982. A memoir of a happy childhood in a prewar peasant village that includes stories of heroic, loyal water buffalo, snakes, and village customs.

David K. Wright, *Vietnam: The Enchantment of the World.* Chicago: Childrens Press, 1989. An overview of Vietnam including history, famous people, and culture.

Michael S. Yamashita, *Mekong: Journey on the Mother of Waters.* New York: Takarajima, 1995. A look at the Mekong's source and journey to the Mekong Delta of Vietnam. Excellent text and photography show the great river's effect on those who live and work on and beside it.

WORKS CONSULTED

Books

Lady Borton, *After Sorrow: An American Among the Vietnamese*. New York: Kodansha America, 1996. Borton has worked with the American Friends Service Committee and lived with Vietnamese off and on for thirty years. She recounts conversations and events that transpire during recent stays in Vietnam.

Susan Brownmiller, *Seeing Vietnam: Encounters of the Road and Heart*. New York: HarperCollins, 1994. A journalist recounts experiences while traveling in the reopened postwar cities and countryside of Vietnam.

Chanoff and Doan Van Toai, *Vietnam: A Portrait of Its People at War*. London: Tauris, 1996. The tenacity and techniques of the Vietnamese during war and the traumatic effects of war on a people.

Geoffrey Clifford, photography, and John Balaban, text, *Vietnam: The Land We Never Knew*. San Francisco: Chronicle Books, 1989. A book of fascinating photographs and informative text about everyday life in Vietnam.

Edward Doyle and Terrence Maitland, *The Aftermath: 1975–85*. Boston: Boston Publishing, 1985. Chronicles the decade following the U.S. troop withdrawal from Vietnam.

Neil L. Jamieson, *Understanding Vietnam*. Berkeley and Los Angeles: University of California Press, 1993. A study of modern Vietnam, particularly from the standpoint of an ancient culture confronting revolution.

John R. Jones, *Guide to Vietnam*. 2nd ed. UK: Bradt Publications, 1994. Informative information for travelers.

Henry Kamm, *Dragon Ascending: Vietnam and the Vietnamese*. New York: Arcade, 1996. An insightful analysis of modern Vietnam by a Pulitzer Prize–winning senior foreign correspondent for the *New York Times*.

103

Stanley Karnow, *Vietnam: A History*. New York: Viking, 1983. Karnow thoroughly details Vietnam's struggles against China and France and focuses on its war with the United States.

Natasha Lesser, ed., *Fodor's Vietnam*. New York: Random House, 1998. A guidebook for travelers who want basic information about the culture of Vietnam and what to expect there.

Robert Emmet Long, ed., *Vietnam Ten Years After*. New York: Wilson, 1986. A look at Vietnam while it remained a closed society.

Nguyen Du, *The Tale of Kieu*. Trans. Huynh Sanh Thong with a historical essay by Alexander B. Woodside. New Haven, CT: Yale University Press, 1983. A lyric translation of the beloved epic. The Woodside essay is a scholarly look at cultural influences on the author as well as a literary criticism of the work itself.

Nguyen Van Canh, *Vietnam Under Communism, 1975–1982*. Stanford: Hoover Press Publications, 1983. A detailed and well-documented history of the first years of communist leadership following reunification of Vietnam.

Norman Podhoretz, *Why We Were in Vietnam*. New York: Simon and Schuster, 1982. Explores how and why America intervened in Vietnam's affairs.

Daniel Robinson and Robert Storey, *Vietnam: A Survival Kit*. Hawthorne, Vic, Australia: Lonely Planet, 1993. A comprehensive guide to Vietnam for the independent traveler.

Robert Scigliano, *South Vietnam: Nation Under Stress*. Boston: Houghton Mifflin, 1963. A detailed look at economic problems of South Vietnam in the early 1960s.

Barry Turner, ed., *The Statesman's Yearbook: The Essential Political and Economic Guide to All the Countries of the World*. New York: St. Martin's, 1998. Current facts about Vietnam.

Periodicals

Lisa Spivey and Albert Wen, eds., *Destination: Vietnam*. San Francisco: Global Directions, March/April 1996, November/December 1996, and January/February 1997.

May Ly Quang, *Vietnam Cultural Window: Special Issue on the Vietnamese Lunar New Year*. Hanoi: Giay, October 24, 1997.

Dick Van, "The Parallel Sentences," *Vietnam, Cultural Window*. Hanoi: Giay, October 24, 1997.

Pamphlets and Booklets

Richard F. Newcomb, *What You Should Know About Vietnam*. Associated Press, 1967.

Welcome to Vietnam. Hanoi: The GIOI Publishers. Document provided by Vietnam delegation to the United Nations.

Internet Sources

Barbara Cohen, "Celebrating Mid Autumn Children's Festival," *Destination Vietnam*, September/October 1995. www.destinationvietnam.com

———, "Shuttlecock," *Destination Vietnam*, May/June 1995. www.destinationvietnam.com

Fernando del Mundo, "Europe: The Debate over Asylum," *Refugees Magazine* 113, 1999. www.unhcr.ch/pubs/rm 113/rm1310.htm

Claire Ellis, "Ao Dai, the National Costume," *Destination Vietnam*, March/April 1996. www.destinationvietnam.com

———, "The History and Mystery of Ceramics," *Destination Vietnam*, July/August 1997. www.destinationvietnam.com

"The Mangrove Ecosystem," Impact on Vietnam. Based on material provided by Professor Phan Nguyen Hong, Director, Mangrove Ecosystem Research Centre, Hanoi National Pedagogic University. www.cru.uea.ac.uk/cru/tiempo/vietnam/impact8htm

Alfredo Quarto and Kate Cissna, "The Mangrove Action Project," Ramsar Convention on Wetlands, November 10, 1997. www.iucm.org/themes/ramsar/about-mangrove-project.htm

Sarah Tilton, "Paper Street," *Destination Vietnam*, March/April 1997. www.destinationvietnam.com

Websites

ASEANWEB (http://vietnam.tdb.gov.svn-inves.html). Promotes investment in Vietnam, providing information about *doi moi*, legislation, and other investment concerns.

Center for Trade with Vietnam (www.freeyellow.com). The site's purpose is to provide a business resource for development of international trade opportunities with Vietnam. It also advocates the normalization of trade relations between the United States and Vietnam.

EBSCOhost Full Display (http://gw10.epnet.com). Background Notes: Vietnam, October 1998; Released by the Bureau of East Asian and Pacific Affairs; U.S. Department of State.

Nam Phuong Gallery (www.namphounggallery.com). Description of art and brief biographical material about artists whose work the gallery exhibits.

UNHCR Country Profiles – Viet Nam (www.unhcr.ch/world/asia/vietnam.htm). Updates on activities of the United Nations High Commissioner of Refugees.

USIA: U.S.-Vietnam Relations (www.usia.gov). Provides information on subjects affecting U.S.-Vietnam relations.

INDEX

PICTURE CREDITS

ABOUT THE AUTHOR

Karen Wills has practiced law and taught writing courses at the college level, and is a freelance writer of fiction and non-fiction. Besides writing, she loves to hike and cross country ski in Glacier National Park near her home. She is an active advocate for the preservation of America's wilderness areas. She has a grown son and daughter. Her master's degree in English and her Juris Doctor are both from the University of North Dakota.